The Mysterious Story of God

Dinesh Sastry

LifeRich PUBLISHING®

LifeRich Publishing is a registered trademark of The Reader's Digest Association, Inc.

LifeRich Publishing books may be ordered through booksellers or by contacting:

LifeRich Publishing
1663 Liberty Drive
Bloomington, IN 47403
www.liferichpublishing.com
1 (888) 238-8637

ISBN: 978-1-4897-2573-8 (sc)
ISBN: 978-1-4897-2571-4 (hc)
ISBN: 978-1-4897-2572-1 (e)

Library of Congress Control Number: 2019919657

Print information available on the last page.

LifeRich Publishing rev. date: 11/29/2019

Absolute Truths and Important Revelations

Dedications

I would like to dedicate this book to the loving memory of my father Durvasula Venkata Sastry, who was my inspiration, my mentor, and my guide. His pioneering works in the Indian-American community are legendary as his involvement in founding and building and running the iconic Shiva Vishnu Hindu Temple in Livermore, California.

I also thank his brothers Durvasula Chanti and the memory of his father, Durvasula Venkata Subbarao for inspiring my political activism in both United States and India.

I would like to also dedicate this book to my father's brothers, Vedantam Durvasula and Prasad Durvasula who guided me intellectually and spiritually respectively. I would like to thank my mother and her large family for all the support they have provided over the decades both in the USA and India. This includes the loving memory of my maternal grandfather Krovi Balakrishnarao.

It would not be complete not to thank all of my friends, both male and female, that have been doing God's work over the decades with extreme patience and without complaints. I also dedicate this work to Jay Gumm my developmental editor from Rockwell, Texas for his patience and precise work on my book, adding structure to my prose.

Finally I would like to thank my other hero in Politics, Spiritual inquisitiveness and life, Gov. Edmund G. "Jerry" Brown, Jr.

CHAPTER 1

Introductions

After visiting more than 500 important religious sites and related historical places, and studying more than 1000 religious, theological, and related historical, anthropological, and archaeological texts, periodicals, and scriptures, and years of careful and intense meditation I have reached some important revelations and things I consider to be absolute truths. It is important to note that some of the temples I have visited are between 7,000 and 10,000 years old, predating Christianity, Islam, Judaism, and conventional Hinduism by several thousand years. In fact, some of these sites predate all organized religions on Earth except for Lord Shiva worship. I have buttressed this research with occasional interactions with members of the world's most powerful and knowledgeable intelligence agencies, secret societies, gurus, swamis, priests, and religious leaders.

This information may be shared with open-minded persons of faith who are somewhat in the know of what has been happening over the past few years. Always remember that the mystery of God is like a complex puzzle, using codes that only one person in the history of time and humanity, with the key to scroll, can solve completely. It is important to know that various scriptures do not read like logically or sequentially constructed narratives but more like a series of bullet points often depicting events that take place out of sequence. However, ultimately, the story of God will be a satisfying and fairly logical narrative.

Important Revelations and Truths:

A trained lawyer may read the Biblical book of Revelations and conclude that the Lamb and God could either be one and the same person or be read as being two separate persons or entities. Similarly, the Vishnu Purana and Kalki Purana can be read to be one Kalki Avatar, or perhaps two separate Kalki avatars separated by time. Similarly, a discussion of the "Counselor" and the Spirit of the Truth" (John 14:26 NIV) mentioned by Jesus Christ would lead one to believe that they are one-in-the-same person. However, there is a loophole for possibility that the Spirit of the Truth and the Counselor are two different entities. This was done to allow the creators to decide how they wanted to solve the puzzle or mystery of God at the appropriate time or end times or end of the Kali Yuga. In other words, it is the choice of the Lion from the Tribe of Judah, the Lamb, the Kalki Avatar, and the Son of Man to decide whether to bifurcate in these situations or refer to one person.

Subsequently it follows that:

- GOD is Durvasula Venkata Subba Rao, grandfather of the Lamb and thus partially Lord Shiva, partially Lord Vishnu, and partially Lord Brahma.
- The Lamb is the son of man, Lion from the tribe of Judah, or Lord RAM (the male sheep or son of Hezron, and Great Grandson of Judah, the second coming of Jesus Christ, the Messiah, the Son of Manu, and Lord Vishnu. He is also Partially Lord Shiva, and Partially Lord Brahma. When the Sprits of Lord Shiva and Lord Brahma are completely upon the Lamb, the Lamb is also Lord GOD Almighty/Allah.
- The Counselor is Durvasula Venkata Subba Rao, hereinafter D. V. Subba Rao. It is rumored that D. V. Subba Rao was the primary secret counselor to both Mahatma Gandhi and Dr. Martin Luther King, Jr.
- The Spirit of the Truth is Mohandas Karamchand Gandhi or "Mahatma" Gandhi.
- The Holy Trinity is the
  o Father-Lord Shiva,
  o The Son-Lord Vishnu, and
  o The Holy Spirit-Lord Brahma.
- Lord Shiva, the destroyer is the Father and represents a "Leopard" because he is often depicted in a leopard dress or loongi, and he has

many crowns on his head as he holds many titles and wears his hair in many buns that resemble crowns. Lord Siva like other Hindu Gods is often depicted by many heads and many arms because he can manifest as or in more than one person at the same space and same time or at different times and spaces.

Lord Shiva and his wife Parvathi also have a "Book of Life" in which Lord Shiva, at the beginning of time, narrates the life story and various truths about every single human being in history. The sages that witnessed his narration to his wife wrote them down in leaves. These leaves are called the Shiva Nadi Shastras. They are found in the Indian state of Tamil Nadu and many of the Nadi Leaves were translated from Sanskrit to Tamil and Telugu languages several thousands of years ago.

Governor Elihu Yale of the Madras Province (now Tamil Nadu and Andhra Pradesh states), who was the most corrupt and brutal official of the British East India company and British Raj, is rumored to have stolen many of these leaves with Christian names and later handed them to secret societies. Yale University in Connecticut, USA is named after Governor Yale, who assisted in the founding of the university. It is also rumored that secret societies are able to use these leaves to recruit potentially powerful and talented members after reading their leaves. However, technically, you cannot match the leaves without the thumbprints of the person for whom they are written along with some other corroborating information.

Thus, the Lamb is Lord Shiva but also Lord Ram (like a male sheep) who is son of Manu/Man and incarnate of Lord Vishnu as state in Vishnu Purana. Both Lord Shiva and Lord Vishnu have incarnated as the Lamb/Son of Man. Similarly, Lord Venkateshwara worshipped in Andhra Pradesh is officially thought to be Lord Vishnu looking for his wife, Goddess Lakshmi. However, the Lord Vishnu aspect of Lord Venkateshwara is represented by his official story and his name, "VENKATA" that means VISHNU. On the other hand, the Lord Shiva aspect of Venkateshwara is represented by ESHWARA in the name. The moniker "Eshwara" usually refers to Lord Shiva. Shambala the symbolic ancient Kingdom prophesied in Buddhist and Hindu prophecies and also the home of the Lamb is bifurcated into two areas. One Shambala is the Peddapuram, East Godavari region of Andhra Pradesh, India where Gautama Buddha recited the Kalachakra Tantra and where parts of the Ramayanam and Mahabharata took place, and where Lord Venkateshwara briefly resided. The other Shambala is in the San Francisco Bay Area in

California, USA where the Lamb was born.

Idol Worship is apparently the troubling issues that prevents all religions from neatly coming together. Jesus Christ, in the Book of Revelations, states that we should worship idols that do not walk, breathe, see, or hear. However, the idols that represent deities that are indeed alive and walking, seeing, hearing, and breathing are appropriately worshipped by Hindus. It will be proven in the near future that all such idols are representing living entities.

Identity of Important Prophets, Saints, Demigods, (both Small and Great)

- Prophet Moses was reincarnated as President John Fitzgerald Kennedy.
- Prophet John the Baptist, Prophet Mohammed, and Prophet Guru Nanak all are reincarnated as Gov. Edmund G. "Jerry" Brown, Jr.
- Prophet Elijah is reincarnated as President William Jefferson Clinton.
- Prophet Elisha is reincarnated as Vice President Albert Gore II.
- Saint John is reincarnated as President George W. Bush.
- Prophet Abraham was reincarnated as President Abraham Lincoln.
- King Solomon was reincarnated as President Ronald W. Reagan.
- King Samuel is reincarnated as President George H. W. Bush.
- Saint Thomas is reincarnated as President James "Jimmy" Carter.
- Other prophets and Saints who were victimized by Mystery Babylon: Senator Diane Feinstein

When I was born in San Francisco, in the French Hospital delivered by Dr. Ruth Christ, my parents took me home to a building owned by Gina Moscone and her mother. I lived there for the first four years of life. Mayor George Moscone became my father's friend, and his children took me trick-or-treating on Halloween. Gina and family convinced my cavalier father to finally buy a house in Pacifica and move out of the building when my mother was pregnant with my brother. My father threw a legendary party in honor of the new home, a housewarming party which nicely coincided with President Nixon's resignation and my brother's birth. It was August 1974.

In 1978, my mother, brother, and I went to Pittsburg, Pennsylvania and Morgantown, West Virginia for Thanksgiving and our annual family reunion. My father stayed back as he had to work at San Francisco

International Airport to clear holiday-scheduled United Airlines aircraft for travel. At the end of the holiday he picked us up at the airport and drove us home to Pacifica. However, before taking the exit to Pacifica, I noticed a ceremony at the Holy Cross Catholic Cemetery in Colma, with something like a 21-gun salute. My dad quietly said, "Yeah, George Moscone was assassinated, and Diane Feinstein is mayor now." My mom was shocked! The Moscones were our friends. Gina and her mother were mentors to my mother since age 19. It was sad for our family.

In 1984 the Democratic National Convention (DNC) was in San Francisco at the George Moscone Center. My dad was selected as an alternate delegate to the DNC. I was already interested in Democratic politics by that time, but my Dad interestingly sent my brother and me to Philadelphia to the Dantaluri Family to spend the summer holidays and to improve our tennis skills as well. My dad was a great tennis player and taught me how to play.

- Robert F. Kennedy, Dr. Martin Luther King, Jr., Malcolm X, Hindu Demigods, and prophets and Saints:
  - The Five Pandava Brothers of the Mahabharata:
    - Akella Krishna Sastry.
    - Vedantam Durvasula.
    - Kalyan Durvasula.
    - Durvasula Satynaranya Murthy (aka Chanti).
    - Prasad Durvasula.
  - King Vasu Deva is Durvasula Sastry.
  - Lakshmana, brother of Lord Ram is Manoj Sastry.
  - Shatrughna, brother of Lord Ram is Sudhir Durvasula.
  - Bharata, brother of Lord Ram is Prashanth Kolluri.
  - Bheema, cousin of Lord Krishna is Kalyan Durvasula.
  - King Dasaratha, father of Ram and formerly Svayambhuva Manu, is my father, D. V. Sastry.
  - Kausilya and The Virgin Mary, the mother of Ram and Jesus respectively is Lakshmi Sastry (my mother).

Shirdi Sai Baba was an incarnation of Lord Brahma who was never worshipped and thus used this loophole. He also wanted to live life briefly as a Muslim for four years and even tasted beef as a child to show that Brahma was no longer masquerading among the calves as he had done briefly to aide Lord Krishna.

- Sage Vashistha is reincarnated as Sri Satya Sai Baba of Puthaparathi.
- Sage ViswaMitra is reincarnated as Sri Viswayogee Viswamjee of Guntur.
- The Father of Arjun, Bheem, and Yuddhistra is Durvasa MahaRishi.
- Durvasua Maharishi is D. V. Subba Rao. Durvasa is ancient qualified Brahmin name.
    o Durvasula is same as "David" for purposes of Revelations and thus the "Root and Offspring of David" is the offspring of Durvasula.
    o The three ELDER brothers of the Kalki avatar as prophesied in Kalki Purana are Ram Akella, Raman Akella, and Bala Akella.
- The Four Living Creatures are creatures though to not exist or thought to have died but are ACTUALLY LIVING!
    o God, D. V. Subba Rao (in Himalayas/China)
    o Lord Hanuman (in Himalayas in original form)(face like a man)
    o Lord Subbarmanyam/Satynarayna swami (son of Shiva) (Duvasula Chanti-my Uncle-also Himalayas /China)(face like an ox)
    o Lord Ganesha, son of Shiva (D. V. Sastry) (Face like a lion)

However, since Lamb and God have been bifurcated, God will be replaced by John the Baptist, Edmund G. Brown, Jr., whose face is like a flying Eagle.

24 Elders: 24 Prominent Elders in History that impress both Lamb and God.

They were originally intended to be the 24 U. S. A. presidents after Abraham Lincoln ended slavery, but that has changed a bit.

- The Eighth King: Guess
- The Seventh King: Guess
- The Bride of the Lamb: The incarnation of Lakshmi Devi or Parvathi Devi, or Goddess Lakshmi as described in the Padma Purana.

- The lamb/Son of Man must eventually marry all former wives in past lives who were all Goddesses such as Saraswati, Parvathi, Rukmini, Jambavathi, Shakti, Gayatri etc. but this is not required to fulfill any prophecies.
- Goddess Durga, like mother Earth and Lalita Devi is my grandmother, Durvasula Atchuthamba, wife of D. V. Subba Rao.
- Springs of Living Water: This is divine or mystical water called Soma in ancient times. It will taste like a divine and heavenly substance pleasing all who drink. The reason that it is described as "Living Water" (John 7:38 NIV) and Jesus Christ says you must eat and drink my "blood and flesh" (John 6:54 NIV) for eternal life is that this is actually the divine semen of Lord Shiva. This is why worship of stone Siva Lingams is more than 10,000 years old. There will be two divine Shiva Lingams, one for God and one for the Lamb and those offered as first\fruits to the Lamb and God will drink the soma and receive eternal life. Men and women will drink the water or soma in the form of champagne or champagne cocktails or juices and much later springs will be formed. Men will actually ask women in the family to pray for them for certain types of extraordinary boons, as this will empower women. When you actually experience it, at that time, it will not be as disgusting or strange as the written description sounds. However, this is how it must be. The water will be offered only after tests of faith have been passed by the worshippers. There will be no deceit or manipulation of the Lamb or God.
- The Followers of the Lamb: The 144,000 (only a symbolic number and not followed) thousand who sing mysterious songs can be interpreted to be Vedic Priests who wear the Tilak or sign of Lord Shiva or Lord Vishnu on their forehead or combination of both (thereby becoming a "Cross" symbol) and chant complex mantras. However, since the Lamb and God decide the definitions, they will be mostly various women who will sing songs or give speeches etc. and be hired to follow The Lamb on occasion in the early years. They will follow the Lamb and not God and not necessarily be offered as first fruits to the Lamb. God will have followers also. The angels of the Lamb will process applications for these very well paid, dignified, and powerful slots. Some will be volunteers by choice. They will not be delegated to any other menial duties and not be shared with any other gods etc. Among them will be some of the

most famous and successful female entertainers (meaning they are popular among men) who may be falsely in trouble, in contrived trouble, or under unfair scrutiny but are blameless and tell no lies.

- Master and Talents and Servants. Throughout the world, front companies, shell companies, equity funds, and financial institutions are managing money/assets and business ideas of the Lamb and God. When the Lamb/Son of Man/MASTER comes back, he will reward the managers who have done well and fairly and punish those like Ken Lay and Bernie Ebbers who have beaten on their servants in a wicked way or used the assets in a wicket way. The lamb and God also secretly have several hundred Patents, Trademarks, and Copyrights that receive royalties.

- Angels of God. Described in various texts, these angels are extensions of Lord God Almighty, the Father and Holy Spirit and represent the powers that the Kalki avatar or the Lamb/son of Man has delegated to the Sprit while he is finishing his human life before entering his permanent divine life. They take orders form the lamb, think exactly as the lamb unless given other duties and can manifest as humans, animals, or even inanimate objects. They do not need food, money, or shelter though some live as humans for example in the intelligence agencies or corporations or hospitals or as robot-type of space fillers representing the extremes of society. Some angels live as the extreme poor, or the very violent, or the extreme rich or very Greedy etc. They will disappear when the Kingdom of God begins. Others will work directly for the Lamb and God.

The New Jerusalem, Heaven on Earth and the Kingdom of God The mistreatment of God and Lamb by various institutions and agencies has guaranteed that the New Jerusalem will be in Peddapuram, East Godavari region (including Kakinada and Rajamundry), Andhra Pradesh, India. Land will expand into the Sea and entire area will be transformed. There will be no question that it was designed by the Lamb and God as it will have various shrines to the favorite athletes and cultural heroes of the God and Lamb. It will resemble San Francisco, and small parts of:

- (The Lamb/Son of Man or his family have visited or touched ground in a majority of the places hereinafter listed): Las Vegas, Nevada; New York City, New York; Mumbai, Maharashtra, India; Hyderabad,

Andhra Pradesh, India; Dublin, Ireland; Scotland; Paris, France; London, England; New Orleans, LA; Rio de Janeiro, Brazil; Seattle, Washington; Chicago, Illinois; Washington DC; Trivanduram, Kerala, India; Kovalam Beach, Kerala, India; Kanya Kumari and Madras, Tamil Nadu, India; Calcutta, West Bengal, India; Bangkok, Thailand; Hong Kong, China; Beijing, China; Moscow, Russia; Geneva, Switzerland; Amsterdam, Holland; Alexandria, Virginia; New Delhi, India; Goa, India; Singapore; Honolulu, Hawaii; Maui, Hawaii; American Samoa; Samoa; Guam; Tokyo, Japan; Bangalore, Karnataka; Los Angeles, CA; Charlotte, North Carolina; Lisbon, Portugal; Kaula Lampur, Malaysia; Greensboro, North Carolina; Charleston, South Carolina; Myrtle Beach, South Carolina; Hilton Head, South Carolina; Oakland, CA; Pacifica, CA; Daly City, CA; Little Rock, Arkansas; Vail, Colorado; Philadelphia, Pennsylvania; Palm Springs, CA; San Diego, CA; Kathmandu, Nepal; Bhutan, Palau; Panama City; Boston, Massachusetts; Orange Beach, Alabama; Fair Hope and Daphne, Alabama; Agra, Uttar Pradesh; Jaipur, Rajasthan; Boise, Idaho; Oklahoma City, Oklahoma; Provo, Utah; Phoenix, AZ (solar and computerized houses); San Antonio, TX; Barcelona, Spain; Montana; Wyoming; Belarus; Nagasaki, Japan; Hiroshima, Japan; Buenos Aires, Argentina; Kokomo, Indiana (largest swimming pool in world); Karachi, Pakistan; Puerto Vallarta, Mexico; Yemen; Puerto Rico; Anchorage, Alaska; Georgetown, Guyana; Santa Barbara, California; Napa Valley, California; Abu Dhabi, United Arab Emirates; Qatar; Dubai; Ramallah, Jordan; Buffalo, (Niagara Falls) New York; Manhattan, New York; Manilla, Philippines; Destin, Florida; Haiti; Copenhagen, Denmark; Brussels, Belgium; Ramstein, Germany; South Dakota; Fargo, North Dakota; Muscat, Amman; The Netherlands; New Zealand; Denmark; Oslo, Norway; Mauritius (Port Louis etc.) Africa; The Czech Republic; Slovakia; Ahmedabad; Gujarat; Berlin, Germany; Botswana; Pearl Harbor, Oahu, Hawaii; Vancouver, Canada; Toronto, Canada; Zimbabwe, Africa; Mozambique, Africa; Houston, Texas; Dallas, Texas; Pyongyang, North Korea; Jakarta, Indonesia; Pittsburgh, Pennsylvania; The Fiji Islands; Trinidad and Tobago, The Virgin Islands; Tehran, Iran; Kabul, Afghanistan; Tibet, Uzbekistan; Disney World/Orlando, Florida; Anaheim, CA; Malawi, Poland; Lithuania; Austria; Romania; Serbia; Croatia; Azerbaijan; Turkmenistan;

Kazakhstan; Macedonia; Republic of Georgia; Hazard, Kentucky; Stockholm, Sweden; Finland; Kenner, Louisiana; Metairie, Louisiana; Baton Rouge, Louisiana; Anchorage, Alaska; Sri Lanka; Sardinia; Kingston, Jamaica; Greenbelt, Maryland; Baltimore, Maryland; Aruba, Bermuda; Cayman Islands; Belize; Managua, Nicaragua; Budapest, Hungary; Chile; Lima; Peru; Bolivia; Bangladesh; Toronto, Canada; Montpellier, Vermont; Bangor, Maine; Chandigarh, Punjab; Costa Rica; Johannesburg, South Africa; Sidney, Australia; Havana, Cuba; Lagos; Nigeria; Frankfurt, Germany; Sausalito, California; Monterey/Pebble Beach, California; Carmel, CA; Discovery Bay, CA; Pleasanton, CA; Fremont, CA; Lake Tahoe, CA/NV; Berkeley, California; Mobile, Alabama; Biloxi, Mississippi; New Jersey; Nashville, Tennessee; Memphis, Tennessee; Tunisia; Africa, Darfur and Khartoum, Sudan; Chad, Somalia; Ethiopia; Paraguay; Ecuador; Uruguay; Caracas, Venezuela; the Ukraine, Latvia, Kenya, The Serengeti; Tanzania; Zambia; New Hampshire; Milwaukee, Wisconsin; Madison, Wisconsin; Mequon, WI; Minneapolis, Minnesota; San Paulo, Brazil; St. Paul, Minnesota; St. Louis, Missouri; Detroit, Michigan; Antarctica; The North Pole (lost civilization); The South Pole (lost civilization); Seoul, South Korea; San Salvador, El Salvador; Estonia; Des Moines, Iowa; Portland, Oregon; The Bahamas; Dominican Republic; Greenland; Tai Taipei, Taiwan; Grenada; Kuwait; Bahrain; Barbados and other Caribbean Islands; Taiwan; Santa Fe, New Mexico; Rehoboth Beach, Delaware; Newport Beach, Rhode Island; Siberia; Guatemala; Lebanon; Burma/Myanmar; Yugoslavia; The Congo; Bosnia & Herzegovina; Kosovo; Uzbekistan; Morgantown, West Virginia; Austin, Texas; Houston, TX; Simla, Kashmir, India; New Haven, Connecticut; Topeka, Kansas; Wichita, Kansas; Omaha, Nebraska; Atlanta, Georgia (Buckhead); Riverdale, Georgia; College Park, Georgia; Columbus, Ohio; Algeria, Tunisia; Morocco; Iceland; Syria; Riyadh, Saudi Arabia; Honduras; Cincinnati, Ohio; Cleveland, Ohio; Libya; Rome, Italy; Venice, Italy; Jerusalem, Israel; Cairo, Egypt; Istanbul, Turkey; Armenia; Athens, Greece; Palestine; Bagdad (or Babylonia) Iraq; and other famous cities and smaller communities that have impacted the designs of the Lamb and God.

CHAPTER 2
Heaven on Earth

There will be a feeling of Heaven on Earth there, and it will be obvious that it is the Kingdom of God. All world governments will be administered directly or indirectly by the Lamb and God from the New Jerusalem. All funding throughout the world of governments will be done from there as taxes will be very low. There will be some appropriate and effect form of guaranteed Living Wages for workers. There will be Democracy at local levels around the world but to ensure near perfection in Government, many major leaders will be appointed. Angels of God who can read minds, perform miracles, anticipate future events and read the future will supplement emergency services such as Fire, Rescue, and Police and Criminal Justices and Hospitals throughout the world in order to prevent crying and pain and cheating and lying and incompetence. Divine Intelligence briefing will support all world government. Organizations such as the United Nations will exist in order to keep talented persons working and leading. However, a Global Planning Council will be constituted to determine appropriate Divine interventions.

Examples would be to replenish natural resources, changes temperatures, or even fix troublesome and accident-prone intersections and roads that are surrounded by important developments that cannot be razed. The Global Planning Council could also help set standard for the global economy and the attrition rate for the labor force when there is eternal life and good health and contained ageing. For example, does Barry Bonds play outfield with Willie Mays for 500 years or 200 years before his son gets a chance?

The San Francisco Bay Area will be groomed to be a Secondary Kingdom of God in the future.

Characteristics of God when the sprit is completely on him D. V. Subba

Rao who is 6'3" will be 6'5", short hair, dark brown complexion, imposing physique, stunningly handsome, always appearing to be 40-50 years in age, brilliant intellect and improve upon his current 13 fluent languages spoken to speaking all languages on Earth and having various supernatural powers and a Shiva Lingam.

Characteristics of the Lamb when the Spirits are completely on him The Lamb will be 6' 5" inches in height and no longer "LOWER THAN HIS ANGELS," Light brown (same as the current complexion) in complexion, long hair of Shiva, Jesus, and Rama, and Krishna, and speak any language, comprehend all things and have the full powers of creation/destruction/preservation, and omnipotence, omniscience, and omnipresence. He will always have the appearance of a 35-year-old person and have no body odors unless designed to be pleasant odors and have no need for physiological or biological functions that are inconvenient including sleep. He will sleep only for social reasons in order to conform to those around him and with him (e. g. his wife and family). He will have various technology and iron scepters to help him including devices that show him what is happening throughout the world and in the mind of any individual. He will be able to do anything at will and have all powers described by the SAGE Markandeya in the Mahabharata when speaking about the Kalki avatar to Lord Krishna. In this dialogue, it is stated that the "Brahmin boy" will be able to materialize weapons, objects, and even armies at will. The Lamb will be devoid of any physiological, neurological, circulatory, or digestive systems. He will be unable to be harmed or incapacitated in any way. He will be able to control the appearance of his children or any children etc. as the creator can, disregarding genetics on occasion. He will be able to pull the file on any problem or any human being on earth and tackle it.

The Lamb will be able to create life, take away life, assign persons to Hell (Lake of Burning Sulfur) and resurrect life independent of Karma. Currently, most life and death and other significant events is decided by a person's Karma (destiny and fate both predetermined and adjusted for prayers and good deeds) in past and present life, however in some cases there are interventions in order to fulfill prophecies.

Day of Lord or Time of Lord

Like a perfectly made computer program, the preset criteria and conditions set by the Lamb and partially by God will be used to eliminate approximately 40%-60% of the World's population in a rapture type of sudden event. The remaining persons will be welcomed into the Kingdom of God and asked to follow divine rules for maintaining eternal life in exchange for losing the right to be evil, right to be harmfully inaccurate or incompetent, and right to be greedy. Some of those who disappear will rest from their labors and they will simply disintegrate. Others are angels and will simply leave like robots. They "do not love their lives so much as to shrink from death" (Revelation 12:11 NIV) because they are robots such as filthy persons, sexually immoral, murderers, thieves, and practitioners of magic arts. They do not have actual souls to punish but are actually filling space and used as props or teaching tools. Those who are actually punished will burn in the lake of burning sulfur forever and burn every single day and will never receive a rest from the eternal suffering and burning. To this date, no person has ever burned in Hell, waiting for the Lamb to decide. The Lamb as the King of Kings and Lord of Lords will then decide either personally or through automated decision making how each and every person is punished. So theoretically, Genghis Khan, Pol Pot, and Adolf Hitler, Kenneth Lay, Bernie Ebbers, Jeffrey Dahmer, Richard Allen Davis, and Dr. P. B. Ram Reddy (former NSA employee) time and next to each other. So, people will be marrying and giving in marriage, eating and being merry and then suddenly a rapture will take away some like a flood.

The Resurrection

This will be the favorite job of the Lamb. Ancient Hindu/Vedic/Brahmin traditions and Celtic traditions taught that a family unit is the Great grandparents down to grandchild and this is similar to how the resurrection will take place in the FLESH and BLOOD. The Resurrected will be miraculously given good health, a bank account, and cell phone among other practical things included a resurrection certificate.

Some Ancient figures such as Kautilya/Chanakya, Chandragupta Maurya, Alexander the Great, Machiavelli, Mahatma Gandhi, U. S. President's Thomas Jefferson, George Washington, Abraham Lincoln, Sun Tzu,

Thomas Edison, Albert Einstein, Winston Churchill, Ferdinand Magellan, Hernando Cortez, Christopher Columbus, Harriet Tubman, Cleopatra, Helen of Troy, King Henry the VIII, Some Kings and Queens who have not been reincarnated and reserved for the resurrection, Julius Caesar, Vasco De Gama, Aristotle, Descartes, Henry David Thoreau, Ernest Hemmingway, Hari Lal Gandhi, President Teddy Roosevelt, Bhagat Singh, Ralph Waldo Emerson, Charles Darwin, Plato, William Shakespeare, Karl Marx, Vladimir Lenin, Scientist J. Robert Oppenheimer, Adam Smith, Josef Stalin, President Richard M. Nixon, King Akbar, Friedrich Nietzsche, Thomas Paine, Tom Sawyer, Agatha Christie, Confucius, Leonardo DaVinci, Frank Sinatra, Babe Ruth, Mark Twain, President George Washington, President Harry Truman, President Dwight D. Eisenhower, George Washington Cleaver, Benjamin Franklin, H. L. Mencken, Marco Polo, Napoleon Bonaparte, and others who impress the Lamb and God will also be resurrected. The oceans will turn to land and uncover lost civilizations and missing pieces to the puzzle of human life. Beaches will remain. This new land will help house some of the resurrected. Supernatural or divine intervention will prevent overpopulation of the Earth. All deadly diseases and sexually transmitted diseases will be eliminated. However, strict rules will be in place though not unusually or uncomfortably strict by the Reasonable person standard in a major suburban area around the present-day world.

Systems of Economy and Government

There will be a hybrid form of Socialism/Capitalism/Monarchy etc. All systems will evolve over time keeping in mind the need for a Utopian society with less iniquities. For example, capitalism can be fair if it plans for the long term and does not put a premium on trimming jobs and overhead but still maintain competition based on quality and not only on financial bottom-line as the financial markets currently require. However, if the master owns most of the capital in circulation, the Master can arbitrarily decide to withstand much higher Price/Earnings ratios without analyzing quarterly developments of a company but actually monitor bi-annual statements and significant events. Thus, a company can provide good jobs with good benefits and not be penalized by the primary stockholders.

Name of the Lamb

The lamb is the SUN and the Light. Thus, the Lamb is named for the SUN. Name of Son of Manu. The Son of Manu is named the Word of God. Examples would be "Sastras" or Revelations etc.

Questions:

1. Why does there seem to be more than one answer for everything? This is a phenomenon explained by Gautama Buddha called "Synchronicity and Coincidence". It occurs to show that something is certainly happening around you even if you miss the first sign or the second sign. It is also meant to distract all but the Lion form the Tribe of Judah with the Key to the scroll from solving the mystery correctly. Thus, it appears that there are many MYSTERY Babylon's but this also signifies that the Kali Yuga or era is ending, and the Kali Yuga is personified in many different ways.

2. What is the Kalki Avatar? The Kalki avatar is one of the originally prophesied and the last incarnation of Vishnu. However, Krishna changed the equation by stating that he would manifest from time to time when the world needed him. Thus, the World needed Jesus Christ and some other limited forms of Vishnu. However, Vishnu is coming one last time and the other two lords, Shiva and Brahma decided to join him. The Kali Yuga is thought to be the most challenging period in the history of humanity requiring Gods that understood the ways of the people, who could outsmart the people at their own game, and use many more powers than previously necessary. The Kalki avatar means the "avatar or incarnation of God for the KALI YUGA". That means he must know economics, politics, warfare, social trends, entertainment, technology, the law etc. "Ki" mean "of" or "for" and "Kal" represents Kali Yuga. Thus, the Kalki avatar must be even more shrewd than Lord Krishna who convinced his own cousin to fight a major war so that the universe could learn some eternal truths and the meaning of life. He must be shrewder than Jesus Christ who was crucified.

3. Why does the Bible seem more accurate than other prophecies? This is because the Prophecies in the bible are more recent in time and more relevant to present conditions and trump some of the older prophecies

that are in conflict. This also reflects the creator's admiration for Jesus Christ and his ability to withstand humiliation and persecution. Also, many of the Kalki Purana prophecies are satisfied by both God and the Lamb in their separate lifetimes. Additionally, nearly all prophecies of all religions are being satisfied by the Lamb and God as there must be a continuous contiguous relationship between the word of God and words of the Messengers of Gods from all religions. If this continuous contiguous relationship is not fulfilled in a satisfactory way, the people lose faith in the word of God, thus all attempts are made to satisfy the word of God. The Word of God in the Biblical Revelations is magnified in importance as Jesus says in Luke 21:33 NIV that "The Heaven and Earth shall pass away, but my words shall not pass away" or "all of these things must Happen," or Revelation 22:18-19 NIV "no one may add a word to this book or take away a word from this book." This is why the Son of Manu must, as stated in Luke 17:22 and Luke 9:22 NIV "suffer many things and be rejected by his generation" as Jesus states but still lead a decent life as is expected in Kalki Purana and Vishnu Purana. Therefore, as stated in Rev. 19: 19 NIV all the "world's armies line up against the rider on the horse" temporarily or the "Beast makes war against the lamb" temporarily, but this ends and the "Lamb wins because he is the King of Kings and Lord of Lords" and with him are "called and chosen faithful "followers, Rev. 14:14 NIV.

4. Does the "practice of Falsehoods" (Revelation 22:15 NIV) refer to lawyers? No, though this is a misconception. It refers to habitual, harmfully manipulative liars.

5. Why are there so many cases against entertainers and athletes the past few years? This is because these strange stories about strange behavior and illegal behavior is not true. The fact is that many people of faith will question why God, D. V. Subba Rao was India's most eminent and leading criminal Lawyer. When it is proven or shown that many of your heroes are innocent, you will be shocked and thank God for good criminal lawyers. Many African-Americans who live with the legacy of slavery have voluntary to allow "them to hate you because of me" as stated by the Holy Spirit in Jesus' words, (Mathew 10:22 NIV). They have chosen to stand on the side of God and suffer until their day comes. The highlights of the Public and secret accomplishments of D. V. Subba

Rao will be so overwhelming and impressive that it will put the whole world into shock and astonishment. Many young entertainers have also been inspired by rumors of his exploits and choose to stand with God and the Lamb. Some cases popularize numbers like 755 and 756 which can be calculated from 666 and some cases show why some DOGS will not make it into the Kingdom of God.

6. Does 9/11/01 calculate from 666? It does if you calculate Boeing 777, Boeing 767, Boeing 757 etc.

7. What is one of the Code Words? The Code word is the first Westerner to climb Mt. Everest in the Himalayas.

8. Are Resurrected persons patiently waiting until others are to join them and the Lamb finally resurrects? Yes, they are patiently waiting. In order to not spoil the surprise and also to allow prophecies to be self-fulfilling, angels of God originally started arranging for some people to artificially be killed and then wait for a Resurrection for Christians and others because there was a doubt that the resurrection might not happen and only reincarnation was possible. Thus, in order to not disappoint Muslims, Christians, and others, some artificial deaths are mixed in, but those majority of those waiting are actually resurrected in flesh and blood. Those whose death may have been staged, did so as show of solidarity with God and Lamb and also in order to satisfy some of the desires and hopes of followers. They are similar to the heroes who are blameless but undergoing media scrutiny or legal scrutiny on behalf of God and Lamb. This is why you see strange stories on cable news or in Iraq of violent deaths, police deaths, hostage deaths, and innocent victim deaths and famous personality deaths.

CHAPTER 3

A Difference

The Democratic Party at least tries to be a moral party despite transgressions of members. They support women without whom there would be no babies and no human beings, you Neanderthals. Who raises children in conservative families around the world? Women do, including in Christian and Islamic families.

Republicans are rallying around serial child predators, and serial sexual predators who are candidates. They also supported Dennis Hastert. Republicans never take responsibility and never resign and never sympathize with women.

Women do not seek to have abortions and do not celebrate them. No one on Earth supports or celebrates late term abortions. This is propaganda devised by evil right-wing political consultants who want to divide the public and maximize the Republican vote. They use Mitch McConnell's money to do this. The late term exception for the health of the mother is religious and moral common sense. There is not a single Evangelical or Conservative or Republican who would let their wife, the mother of his children and his partner and soulmate, to die while having a child if they could prevent it.

A human soul and thus a Destiny and a horoscope is not added to a fetus until it is born and appears out of the womb with the planetary positions carefully recorded at exact time of birth. However, despite this I believe women should decide on an abortion in the first or second trimester and not later for emotional and health reasons unless the Mother's health is at risk.

You know, Lord Krishna like the Lamb (Second Coming of Christ) in the Bhagavad Gita with Krishna's Gopikas and wives and in Revelation 14:4 in the Bible respectively never had to use workplace power or sexual harassment to get women followers. The women just voluntarily followed them around the world because they were Holy and admirable. Many say Krishna, Ram, Rammstein, Ramallah, and Christ were all the same person revealed at different times to different peoples at different periods of time.

I wish people like Politicians would stop implying that they might be "Jesus" or divine beings. They are false prophets. Let them come back down to Earth and drop the Messiah complexes, apologize for their misdeeds, and stop pulling wool over the eyes of the people

CHAPTER 4

Official Prophets and Saints and Key Pieces to Mystery of God

Read the whole document (all questions are answered):

Lord Vishnu was incarnated as Jesus Christ as predicted by Lord Krishna in Chapter 4, Verse 7 of the Bhagad Gita.

Gaius is reincarnated as David Gergen.

Demetrius is reincarnated as Rev. Al Sharpton.

Apollos is reincarnated as President William Jefferson Clinton/Prophet Elijah.

Cephas is reincarnated as Pope Francis who shares the Spirit of Saint Peter, Apostle of Christ.

Eldad was reborn as Bill Maher/Ram Uppuluri.

Medad was reborn as John Meacham.

Lot is reincarnated as Gov. Edmund G. "Jerry" Brown, Jr.,/John the Baptist/Prophet Mohammad/Guru Nanak.

Saint Paul is reincarnated as Barack Obama.

The Apostle and Saint Stephen (the first martyr) was reincarnated as the Late Tim Russert.

Diotrephes is reincarnated as Radio Talk Show host Rush Limbaugh.

Sister Phoebe is reincarnated as Cindy McCain

The Devil, Satan, Dragon, Ancient Serpent, Lucifer, & Gad is Robert S. Mueller, III with help from J. Edgar Hoover & other FBI Directors! This is also a large part of Mystery Babylon the Prostitute Whore!

Mordicai is reincarnated as Secretary of State Warren Christopher.

Haman is reincarnated as President Hasan Rouhani

Saint John is reincarnated as President George W. Bush.

Prophet Elisha is reincarnated as Vice President Albert Gore, Jr.

King Solomon was reincarnated as President Ronald W. Reagan.

Abraham was reincarnated as President Abraham Lincoln.

Herrod Antipas and Moses was reincarnated as President John F. Kennedy.

King David was reincarnated as D.V. Subbarao/Durvasa Maharishi (Lord Siva Incarnation)/Messiah (Also the first thought to be the Lamb/son of Man/kalki avatar in Durvasula Family.)

The Counselor is D. V. Subba Rao, Prophet Mohammed, Bruce Lindsey.

The Spirit of the Truth was Mohandas "Mahatma" Gandhi.

Saint Michael and Joseph is reincarnated as D. V. Sastry/Lord Ganesha/Svayambuva Manu.

Caesar Augustus was reincarnated as President Harry Truman.

Zechariah was reincarnated as Gov. Edmund G. "Pat" Brown.

Miriam is reincarnated as Speaker Nancy Pelosi.

Prophetess Anna is Aretha Franklin.

Gideon was reincarnated as Chief Justice and Gov. Earl Warren.

Methuselah was reincarnated as Senator Robert Byrd.

Saint Thomas in reincarnated as President James "Jimmy" Carter.

Saint Mark is reincarnated as Tony Coelho.

Saint Andrew is reincarnated as Terry McAuliffe.

Saint Simon the Zealot is reincarnated as Sen. John Kerry.

Amos is reincarnated as Sen. Edward "Teddy" Kennedy.

Prophet Joel is Sen. Tom Daschle.

Jonah is reincarnated as Malcolm X.

Saint James is Jeb Bush

Saint James, son of Joseph, is Manoj Sastry/Lakshman.

Bheema is reincarnated as Kalyan Durvasula.

Mary Magdalene was reincarnated as Jennifer Lopez/Mother Theresa.

The Prophet Isaiah is reincarnated as director Michael Moore.

The Prophet Jeremiah is reincarnated as Patrick Caddell.

Aaron is reincarnated as Robert F. Kennedy

Noel is reincarnated as Richard Goodwin

Annas is reincarnated as Secy. Donald Rumsfeld.

Samuel is reincarnated as President George H. W. Bush.

Eli was reincarnated as Sen. Prescott Bush.

Joel the son of Samuel was reborn as Gov. John Kasich

Joshua was reincarnated as President Lyndon Baines Johnson.

Ezra is reincarnated as Ambassador Michael "Mickey" Kantor.

Ezekiel is reincarnated as Mayor Willie Brown of San Francisco who was also longtime Speaker of California state assembly.

Hosea is reincarnated as Baseball Player Barry Bonds.

Micah was reincarnated Sen. Robert F. Kennedy.

The Angel Gabriel is reincarnated as Sen. Dianne Feinstein.

Naomi is reincarnated as Anne Gust Brown, wife of Gov. Edmund G. Brown, Jr.

Orpah is reincarnated as Oprah Winfrey, actress and Television Talk show host and activist.

Jonathan was reincarnated as President and Gen. Dwight D. Eisenhower.

Sarah was reincarnated as First Lady Mary Todd Lincoln.

CHAPTER 5
Kali and the Pregnant Woman

The Discussion of Kali is very completed as she is a Goddess with Multiple personalities and she is the symbol of the Kali Era or Kali Yuga that is about to end. If you research the characteristics of the Kali Era, you will notice that some political, social, and economic and religious trends are obviously bad or evil and will be disposed of but some of the practices or trends will remain in the Era of Truth or Sathya Yuga that will be the Kingdom of God.

Kali, the Hindu Goddess who was jilted at the altar by Lord Shiva because of her violent and destructive activities in the days leading up to their scheduled marriage day. Since then, this consort of Shiva has not been married to Shiva and the Era we are in is called the Kali Era. The Kali Era or Kali Yuga manifest itself as Myster Babylon on a United States government that is largely scarlet and purple because the system has divided various states into Blue States and Red States. Blue States are supposedly Progressive and Democratic and Red States are Conservative and Republican. The country is thus very polarized along party lines and cultural lines. Big Oil companies, the Military Industrial complex, and Big Drug companies seem to control the Kali Yuga and Mystery Babylon and manifest themselves as Republican, neoconservative administrations that are beholden to the lobbyists of these big Corporations and Industrial Sectors and also infiltrate the functioning of Intelligence agencies and law enforcement agencies.

Kali took the two wings of a Great Eagle when my father immigrated to the United States in 1961. President Eisenhower has previously warned about the Military Industrial complex at this time. This gave the story of God an American flavor.

Kali in her benevolent manifestation, became pregnant and screamed in

2000. I was snatched up by God in November 2000 or on Dec. 12, 2000. The two wings of the eagle were actually those of a dove (Al Gore) and a Hawk (Senator Joe Lieberman). Thus, Kali continues to operate as a flip-flopper, taking both the wing of a dove and of a hawk, while both wings are that of the United States symbolic golden eagle.

My mother, Lakshmi Sastry also became pregnant in 1970 and gave birth to the child in 1971 who will rule the nations with an iron scepter. She took the two wings of an eagle in 1970 after marriage in 1969. However, this is also Synchronicity and Coincidence at work and thus, to avoid confusion, my Angels have not allowed her to receive her U. S. Citizenship papers until this was explained properly. However, the term mother alternates between referrals to Lakshmi Sastry and to Kali, almost seamlessly.

My mother is not Kali but Kali and Mystery Babylon can be approximately personified by Condoleezza Rice who sat on the board of Oil Company Chevron, and worked with Unocal and also was instrumental in the Beast out of the Sea and Secretary of State for the Beast out of the Earth. Kali and Mystery Babylon can also be coincidentally personified by Speaker Nancy Pelosi because of her powerful title as Speaker and her ancestry from Rome and her representation of San Francisco. Kali and Myster Babylon can also be personified by Senator Hillary Rodham Clinton as she is representing New York and she and Her husband, President Clinton have travelled all over the world and met with numerous world leaders. She has travelled to more than 82 countries. I participated in her India trip. All three women have ridden the Scarlett and Purple beast to some extent.

Goddess Rukmini is reincarnated as Chelsea Clinton.

King Xerxes is reincarnated as Sen. John McCain.

Barnabas is reincarnated as Eric Holder

Prophet Daniel is reincarnated as Hardip Singh Dosonge.

Saint Jude is reincarnated as Prashant Kolluri.

Simon Magus is reincarnated as commentator and former California Democratic Party Chair, Bill Press, former aide to Gov. Jerry Brown.

Apostle Thaddaeus is reborn as Senator Mark Warner of Virginia.

Bharat is reincarnated as Prashanth Kolluri.

King Josia was reincarnated as President Fidel Castro.

Dharmaraj/Yuddhistir was reincarnated as Akella Krishna Sastry.

Nathan, prophet to King David, was reincarnated as First U. S. Securities and Exchange Commission Chairman, Joe Kennedy (father of President John F. Kennedy).

Titus is reincarnated as United States Senate Majority Leader Harry Reid who praised the Lamb in a Palo Alto, California room full of nine well known Billionaires and 10 U. S. Senators as one of America's rising leaders.

Philemon is reincarnated as Senator Sherrod Brown of Ohio!

Ishmael is reincarnated as King Abdullah II of Jordan.

Jacob, son of Isaac was reincarnated as President Thomas Jefferson of the United States of America.

Cyrus of Persia was reincarnated as President George Washington of the United States of America.

The apostle and Saint Bartholomew is reincarnated as Senator Joe Biden.

The apostle and Saint Phillip is reincarnated as Gov. Andrew Cuomo.

The Prophet Joseph, Son of Jacob & Rachel is Rep. John Lewis.

Menasses is reborn as Ambassador Andrew Young.

Ephraim is reincarnated as CEO Craig L. Davis.

Hagar is reincarnated as Tiffany Caine/Mary J. Blije/Tiffany Hadish/ Taraji P. Henson,/Gabriel Union/Omarosa Manigault, Sally Hemings.

Haggai is reincarnated as Gary Belz, the childhood friend of both President Bill Clinton and Vice President Al Gore.

Obadiah is reincarnated as Peter Knight, advisor to Vice President Al Gore.

Hannah is reborn as Dorothy Walker Bush, wife of Prescott Bush.

Enoch is reincarnated as Adam Kreisel, friend and law classmate of Lamb and former DNC official.

Habakkuk is reincarnated as David Axelrod

Zephaniah is reincarnated as Douglas J. Band, friend and law classmate of Lamb and Counselor to President Bill Clinton.

Prophet Abel was reborn as Secretary Leon Panetta.

Prophet Cain was reborn as CIA Director John Brennan.

Nahum is reincarnated as U. S. Treasury Secretary Robert Rubin.

Isaac, son of Abraham, was reincarnated as San Francisco Police Department officer, the Late Isaac Espinoza, friend of the Lamb.

Essau, son of Isaac in reincarnated as Don Ernst, former education adviser to Gov. Bill Clinton and Gov. Evan Bayh and friend of Lamb.

King Nebuchadnezzar is reincarnated as consumer Activist Ralph Nader.

The great Sage Kripacharya is reincarnated as Dr. Raj Prasad, Retd. Asst. Superintendent of Schools, San Mateo County, CA and advisor to Lamb and others.

The great Sage Dronacharya is Prime Minister Atal Bihari Vajpayee.

The apostle and Saint, James, son of Alpheus was reincarnated as Cesar Chavez, the Civil Rights Leaders and founder of the United Farm Workers of America.

The Saint Timothy is reincarnated as Sen. Bob Kerry

The Brother Simon of Jesus, is Sudhir Durvasula

The Brother of Jesus, Joses (Joseph) is Kalyan Durvasula.

Seshu Peddapudi, Aparna Durvasula, Veena Kolluri, Prasanthi Durvasula Mandalay, and Anuradha Durvasula, and Nagamani (Rani) Chavali are the unnamed sisters of Jesus.

Moabites, wife of King Solomon is reincarnated as First Lady Laura Bush.

Jehu, from the time of King Ahab, is reincarnated as Journalist Bob Woodward.

Jehonadaub, from the time of Jehu, is reincarnated as Journalist Carl Bernstein

A Daughter of King David is reincarnated as Jodie Evans, former aide to Gov. Jerry Brown.

Sage Narada was reincarnated as late Narayan D. Keshavan.

Senator Barbara Boxer is a reincarnation of one of the Daughters of King David.

Michelle Obama is a reincarnation of a one of the Daughters of King David.

King Ahab is reincarnated as President Richard M. Nixon.

Boaz is reincarnated as Sen. Joe Lieberman.

Saint Mathew is reincarnated as Rev. Jessie Jackson.

Saint Luke is reincarnated as Durvasula Satyanarayana Murthy

Job was reincarnated as Rev. Dr. Martin Luther King, Jr.

Saint Peter is reincarnated as Chris Mathews.

Nehemiah, the Jewish "cupbearer" is reincarnated as Dr. Alan Greenspan, former Chairman of the U. S. Federal Reserve.

Baal-Zebub is reincarnated as political strategist and analyst James Carville, advisor to Gov. Bill Clinton.

King Ramses, adopted Brother of Moses, was reincarnated as Prime Minister Jawahrlal Nehru of India.

Jesus Christ's favorite Archangel is Angel Remiel! That Archangel is reborn as Greg Moore of the Rainbow Coalition, Chief of Staff to John Conyers, & DNC Voter Outreach!

Archangel Uriel is Attorney Shan Thever!

Archangel Raphael is Raj Karmakar of Mobile, AL & Houston, TX!

Caleb is reincarnated as Gov Mario Cuomo.

King Ahaziah was reincarnate as President Gerald R. "Jerry" Ford.

Melchizedek is reincarnated as Rev. Billy Graham (also Prophet Malachi).

King Saul was reincarnated as President Woodrow Wilson.

King Adonijah was reincarnated as Prime Minister Sir Winston Churchill.

The Lamb/Son of Man and Jesus Christ and Kalki Avatar/Lord Ram/ Lord Krishna/Lord Venkateshwara/Maitreya/Messiah and representative of and eventual Holy Trinity/Tri Murthy/Dattatreya/Trimbakeshwer/ Ramalingeshwar/Allah/Lord God Almighty is Dinesh Subbaraya Sastry.

The Holy Spirit is Lord Brahma and currently delegated between Angels from Heaven, the Lamb/son of Man and a Holy Spirit. The Father is Lord Shiva and currently delegated between the Angels from Heaven, the Lamb/ Son of Man, and D. V. Subba Rao. The Son of God is Lord Vishnu and is currently delegated between the Lamb/Son of Man and D. V. Subba Rao.

Sirdhi Sai Baba is incarnate of Lord Brahma and is again part of the Tri Murthy, Dinesh Sastry.

Great Sage Kashyap was reincarnated as Krovi Bala Krishna Rao (grandfather of Lamb)

Goddess Aditi was reincarnated as Krovi Mungamma.

Great Sage Vashistha is reincarnated as Sathya Sai Baba of Puttaparthi and Whitefield, India.

Great Sage Viswamitra is reincarnated as Sri Viswayogi Viswamjee of Guntur, India.

Great Sage Bhishma was reincarnated as Prime Minister P. V. Narasimha Rao.

Maharishi Garga is Mallipudi Pallam Raju of Kakinada!

Great Sage Markandeya is reincarnated as Pisappati Veanu Gopaal of Mangalore, India.

Great Sage Brhaspathi was reincarnated as Bhamidipati Krishna Mohan, Former U.P.S.C., India

Sage Dadhichi is reincarnated as Hota Shivaram Sastry (granduncle)

The Great Sage and Saint Bharadwaja was reincarnated as Dr. Romesh Japra of Fremont, CA.

The Great Sage and Saint Atreya was reincarnated as Kalyan Malladi of Kovur, A. P., India.

Lord Satyanarayana are reincarnated as Durvasula Satynarayana Murthy (Chanti and also Donald Trump).

Samson is Donald J. Trump.

Lord Indra is no more.

Goddess Lalitha/Durga is incarnated as Durvasula Atchuthamba, wife of D. V. Subba Rao.

Goddess Shatrupa and Lakshmi Ganapathi is incarnated as Lakshmi Sastry.

The Virgin Mary is reincarnated as Lakshmi Sastry.

St. Elizabeth was reincarnated as Bernice Brown, mother of Gov. Jerry Brown.

King & later Sage Vridhakshatra is Satyanarayana Murthy Kolluri!

Sage BRAMARSHI as is reborn as Krishna Srinivasa of Atlanta!

SAGE Angiras is reborn as Dr. Prasad Annavajhalla.

Suripa Wife of Angiras is Lalitha Annavajhalla.

Utathyasson of Angitas is Kishore Annavjhalla.

Samvartana son of Angiras is Rama Annavajhalla.

Sage Pulastya is reborn as Hota Parthasarathy Sastry!

Saptarishi Marichi is reborn as Durvasula Sriramamurthy from Milwaukee & Michigan.

Dharmavrata/Devashila is reborn as Chanti Hota Durvasula.

Rishi Pulaha is reborn as Pulila Venkat Rao from Peddapuram. His wife is his reborn wife.

Daughter of Pulaha, Kardamma is writer Hota Padmini.

Saptarishi Kratu is Pandit Mallapudi Rama Krishna in Peddapuram, AP, India.

Sage Jagdamani is Hota Sitaram Sastry

Sage Gautama is Ganga Rao Hota!

Ahalya, wife of Gautam Maharishi is Rajeshweri Hota!

Maharishi Shandilya is now Lakshminarayan Sastry Lanka.

The Sage Vyasa is my Cousin Vijay Peddapudi.

The Sage Vidura is my cousin Chavali Ramarao.

Pravahana Jaivali is reborn as Anil Patibandla.

Pinjalaa wife of Vyas is Sirisha Peddapudi!

Subh & Labha are sons of Ganesha. Subh is Vijay Peddapudi. Labha is Sreeram Thyagarajan.

Santoshi Maa daughter of Lord Ganesha is Seshu Peddapudi Thyagarajan.

Ashokasundari/Bala Tripurasundari is Suryamala (Durvasula) Peddapudi.

The Sage Vyasa is my Cousin Vijay Peddapudi.

The unnamed sisters of Jesus are Seshu Peddapudi, Veena Kolluri, Anuradha Durvasula, and Prashanthi Durvasula Mandalay!

Kameswara husband of Tripura Sundari is Peddapudi Ramasastry/Lakshmi Mittal

Shuka child of Vyas is Vikram Peddapudi!

Maharishi Brighu is reborn as high court of AP justice Chavali Somiagulu!

Jagatkaru husband of Manasa is Chavali Narayana Rao/Sheldon Adelson!

Anantha Lakshmi wife of Lord Satyanarayana is Nagamani Chavali Durvasula

Annapurna (Durvasula) Chavali is Manasa!

Jyoti was born as the eldest daughter of DV Subbarao but died in fire!

My maternal Great Grandfather Hota Veerabhadra Swamy is Veerabhadra Swamy husband of Bhadrakali.

Anjana, Daughter of Gautama Maharishi is Lekha Hota (Hinckle)

Vamadeva, Son of Gutama Maharishi is Siva Hota!

Nodhas, son of Gautama Maharishi is Nathan Hinckle!

The children of Draupadi, Sutasoma, Shrutakarma, Satanika are Sommenvita Hota, Sankeerta Hota & Samyutha Hota!

Dushyasan is Veerabhadra Hota (Aka Raja) !

Shrutasena last son of Pandavas is Vishal Thyagarajan!

Prativindhya first son of Panadavas is Sriram Thyagarajan!

The unnamed sisters of Jesus are Seshu Peddapudi, Veena Kolluri, Anuradha Durvasula, and Prashanthi Durvasula Mandalay!

Duhsala only daughter of Dhritarastra (father of Kauravas) is Kamesweri Kolluri!

Nisha Mahimdra Kolluri is Mandavi from Ramayana!

Alia Kolluri is Taksha.

Simran Kolluri is Pushkala.

Jayadratha husband of Duhsala is Sharma Kolluri!

Suratha Jayadrhata is Sai Bhaskar Kolluri!

King & later Sage Vridhakshatra is Satyanarayana Murthy Kolluri!

Subhadra sister of Lord Krishna is Praveena Kolluri!

Dhritastra is Krovi Bala Krishna Rao & Gandaharvi is Hota Mungamma!

When the Trimurthy decided Lord Ganesha would always be worshipped first, Lord Brahma decided to creat a separate "Goddess Shakti for him. He created Budhi (Intellect), Siddhi (Spiritual power) & Riddhi (Prosperity)! All these are Durvasula Ramalakshmi Krovi Sastry my mother.

Vrushali wife of Karna is Reena Patel Krovi!

Bhanumati wife of Duryodhana is Rajeshweri Krovi!

Govindraju, brother of Lord Venkateswara is Vinay Krovi.

Bhudevi is Deepti Krovi!

Balrama elder brother to Lord Krishna & Revati his wife is Gov Edmund G. "Jerry" Brown, Jr. & Anne Gust Brown.

Abhimanyu the son of Arjuna is Medha Akella!

Lord Balaji Mehendipur & of Tirupati who is at side of Lord Venkateswera is Vish Akella and his wife is Meera Akella. Vish is also Sudarshana.

The Kalki Avatar's third eldest brother, Pragya & wife Maalini are Bala Akella & Madhavi Akella.

Their children:

Yagya & Vigya are Neha Akella & Anisha Akella, respectively.

The Kalki Avatar's second eldest brother Pragya & his wife Sumuti is Ram Akella & Sita Akella! Their children Shasan & Vegavaan are Swetha Akella & Abishek Akella, respectively.

The eldest brother of Kalki Avatar Kavi is Raman Akella and his wife is Lakshmi Akella.

Their children Vrihad Keerti Vrihadbahu are Prithvi Akella & Pratima Akella respectively!

Uddalaka Aruni is reborn as Sarma Modali!

Some members of the Durvasula family and Presidents and Vice Presidents of the USA are "Like a Son of Man!" #BibleStudy

My Father Durvasula Venkata Sastry& Gov. Jerry Brown, My Grandfather, DV Subbarao, & I are the Angels from the Church of Philadelphia! They represent honest & powerless Media, Progressive politics, Entertainment, and immigrants.

Lord Kartik/Subbraymanyam is Vinay Prasad Durvasula!

Devasena & Valli the Wives of Lord Kartik are Kanthi Lolla Durvasula

Manikanthan son of Lord Siva is Vedantam Durvasula!

Ayyappa Swamy is Dinesh Subbaraya Sastry.

Madri Devi is Kala Durvasula!

Simon, brother of Jesus, is Sudhir Durvasula!

Lord Agni (fire God) is Ramanjaneylu Swami Vedala of Jackson, Mississippi.

Wife of Lord Sudarshana Chakri, Vijayavalli, is Meera Akella.

Sage Renukacharya is Rompicherulu Sreenivasacharylu.

Sirisha Ganti Durvasula is Shrutakirti the wife of Satrughan.

Shatrughati is Avantika Durvasula

Subahu is Ameya Durvasula

Joses, brother of Jesus, is Kalyan Durvasula!

Vana Durga daughter of Lord Satynarayana is Anuradha Durvasula!

Satyaki, is the late Durvasula Chinna Subbarao! Donald Trump, Jr.

Sushruta is Bandapally Madan Mohan Reddy of Delhi.

Bhaskaracharya or Bhaskar the Second is Arun Ramachandran of Bangalore.

Sage Agnivesa is Krishnamurthy Hari of Walnut Creek, California.

King Muchukunda is born again as Mocherla Bhaskar Rao of San Francisco.

Sage Ahstavakra is Satya Putcha of Mobile, Alabama.

Suprabha, wife of Astavakra is Annapurna Putcha.

CHAPTER 6

The White House of the United States is the Temple of the Lord:

More importantly, there was an interesting incident when Douglas J. Band, in September 2000 listed The Lamb/son of Man and unnamed California businessman as personal guests of President Clinton to a Rose Garden reception for Indian Prime Minister Atal Behari Vajpayee. The Lamb/Son of Man had routinely visited the Old Executive Building and the East Wing of the White House scores of times over several years and even interviewing for jobs there. However, he had not been inside the West Wing offices though dropping friends off several times in the special parking lots.

At this event, a Cabinet Secretary invited the Lamb/Son of man for a small reception of Asian American politicians and appointees with President Clinton and PM Vajpayee after the Rose Garden speeches were finished. The Lamb, the businessman, and others followed the Secretary until the entrance of the drawing room and stood there looking inside for Clinton family members. The Lamb/Son of Man explained to them that as personal guests of the President we could walk in without any problem. However, it was decided to call The relatives of the President later.

The Intelligence agencies saw this on tape and saw that the Lamb/son of Man was measuring the West Wing like an outer court. They proceeded to remove the Lamb/Son of Man's name from special West Wing events like State Dinners and the White House Christmas parties much to the chagrin and surprise of the DNC and other officials. The rumor was floated that First Lady Hillary Clinton or Terry McAuliffe had eliminated the Lamb/Son of Man's name several times. This was not true, as it was a covert decision by the intelligence agencies. This is because it was decided the Lamb/Son of Man should not enter the inner part of the West Wing until the time had come to rule. Similarly, the businessman's name was removed from White House invitation lists as it was not clear to agencies if the businessman was one of the two witnesses, or the Lamb or God or Elijah etc.

In contrast, Vice President Al Gore hosted a spectacular lunch full of prominent people for Prime Minister Vajpayee in the State Department and the Lamb attended and the room was full of guests invited by both the Lamb and Vice President Gore in coordination. At least 30 guests were prominent leaders in various fields recommended by the Lamb.

Also, as King of Kings and Lord of Lords, you will see that the Lamb shares traits with various Kings and Lords including living in Alexandria, VA as did President George Washington.

CHAPTER 7
Two Witnesses and Beast and False Prophet

The **two witnesses**/prophets known figuratively as Sodom and Egypt who terrorized the inhabitants of the Earth are Saddam Hussein and Yasser Arafat, respectively.

Hybrid Economic System That is Sustainable

The economic chain is only as strong as the weakest link. As inequality builds among nations and within nations you approach unrest, revolt, disaffection, and destruction of consumer markets.

Asset Tax to Alleviate Wealth Inequality

As the Republican tax plan is being debated or actually rushed through, we must remember that income inequality and income redistribution are not the issue or major problem. The problem is enormous wealth inequality or disparity.

If there is chaos and mayhem and insecurity in the streets and markets of a nation, the poor and lower middle class will think "Oh well it wasn't that great for us anyway so there isn't much difference, we have nothing to lose."

The wealthy and powerful however would lose everything they valued including the good life and wealth in assets and paper and in markets and their safety on the streets. Thus, the wealthy have an obligation to pay their fair share in wealth in order to maintain and expand their wealth and good life.

Punishing hard earned income and productivity excessively as we do now may not be a fair answer. An asset tax of 3% a year for people with $5 Million or more in assets and eliminations of all income and payroll taxes at federal level may be best and fair way. Economist Daniel Altman has run the numbers and this system brings in the needed revenue. This would not punish hard earned income of common people or slightly well-off people but would force those with the most accumulated assets and thus the most to lose to pay a fair share for national defense, public safety and other services that protect the value of their assets in the long term. This could be called a national security or national integrity tax.

Perhaps this is currently practically unenforceable due to technology and privacy limitations or even unconstitutional but that can change. You can use clever loopholes or have a multi-issue Constitutional Convention.

However in meantime if you tax FICA and Medicare/ Social Security payroll tax on much higher incomes than the current cap at $160,000 or so and also tax passive income than the wealthy who really benefit from the stability of our governments, banks, and institutions and military and law enforcement would surely be paying enough to keep social security and Medicare solvent and reducing our national debt. The people who make $160,000 or less need every penny they earn to live including the regressive flat payroll tax.

https://mobile.nytimes.com/2012/11/19/opinion/to-reduce-inequality-tax-wealth-not-income.html?referer=https://www.google.com/

https://mobile.nytimes.com/2013/02/10/business/yourtaxes/a-wealth-tax-would-look-beyond-income.html?referer=https://www.google.com/

If the disparity between the wealthy and poor begins to expand, you eventually won't have enough consumers to buy products of corporations that maintain the wealth and investments of the haves. The wealthy only buy one or two cars, one or two toothbrushes, a few bars of soap, a smartphone or two, some new clothes and that's it.

There are not enough people in the top 1% of wealth owners to sustain industry sectors and factories or to fund the government with their tax revenues. You need the broad populace to sustain the capitalist economic system.

Absent this there would be a global economic collapse and all assets of the wealthy including gold, real estate, bonds, equities, currencies would diminish in value and cause chaos and mayhem.

The progressives who have tried to address this issue sometimes struggle to find solutions within the capitalist framework. The conservatives do not even consider addressing inequality as an end. They have pandered to the wealthy and corporate lobbyists without dealing with consequences.

Intellectual conservatives like William F. Buckley or Jack Kemp and may have realized the faults and attempted to tweak supply side and laissez-faire economics as well as limited government and developed a necessary hybrid form of economics however they don't address cronyism and need for regulations. Adam Smith did not foresee many of the modern developments and excesses in capitalism and technology.

Not everyone has the interest, talent, greed, or time, opportunity, and capital to try to accumulate huge sums of wealth and yet they must still survive in society and be able to act as consumers as part of the hybrid capitalist system.

An economy with a stock market with equities being afforded high Price to Earnings (P/E) sustained by a middle class of people who are on the average nearly millionaires would support a global, long term, High prosperity, High growth. Experts would point to potential inflation and a dearth of low wage labor if this happens. However, that is why you have robots, angels to do jobs no one wants to do anymore and why, geniuses are appointed to the Federal Reserve and Central Banks worldwide.

We would also need the asset tax on people with enormously large amounts of wealth and replace other regressive or unproductive taxes. This would give large corporations and even many small businesses a good supply of fairly affluent middle-class consumers globally while at the same time allowing the wealthy to increase their hard earned or wisely accumulated or inherited wealth to grow with the public and private markets. This would eventually lead to Utopia with a safety net and pro-competitive legal regime for small businesses.

The False Prophet and the Beast are Osama bin Laden and Al Qaeda/Taliban, respectively.

Goddess Parvathi is incarnated as an identified person.

Goddess Saraswati is incarnated as an identified person.

Goddess Sita reincarnated as an identified person.

Guru Gobind Singh the 10th Guru of the Sikh religion is reincarnated as Prime Minister and Economist Dr. Manmohan Singh, of India.

he Five Pandava Brothers of the Mahabharata: Akella Krishna Sastry, Vedantam Durvasula (Nakula), Kalyan Durvasula, Durvasula Satynaranya Murthy (aka Chanti is Arjuna), and Prasad Durvasula (Sahadeva). King Vasu Deva is Durvasula Sastry.

Balarama (elder brother of Lord Krishna) is Gov. Edmund G. "Jerry' Brown, Jr.

Lakshmana, brother of Lord Ram is Manoj Sastry.

Shatrughna, brother of Lord Ram is Sudhir Durvasula.

Bharata, brother of Lord Ram is Prashanth Kolluri.

Bheema, cousin of Lord Krishna is Kalyan Durvasula.

King Dasaratha father of Ram and formerly Svayambhuva Manu is my father, D. V. Sastry

Kausilya and The Virgin Mary, the mother of Ram and Jesus respectively is Lakshmi Sastry (my mother)

Urmilla, wife of Lakshman is Alejandra Espinosa Sastry.

Sumitra is Kamesweri Krovi Kolluri

Kaikeyi is Kala Durvasula

Four Living Creatures:

1. Lord Ganesha (D. V. Sastry) Face like a lion
2. Lord Hanuman (original eternal Hanuman) face like a man (In Himalayas Mountains)
3. Lord /Satyanarayana (Durvasula Chanti) Face like an ox.
4. Gov. Edmund Gerald "Jerry" Brown, Jr. Face like a flying Eagle.

Martha is reincarnated as Martha Garcia Espinosa, mother-in-law of Manoj Sastry.

Mary, sister of Martha, is reincarnated as Maria Alejandra Garcia Espinosa-Sastry, wife of Manoj Sastry.

Lazarus is reincarnated as Gerardo Garcia Espinosa, son of Martha Espinosa and brother of Alejandra Sastry.

Lava, son of Lord Ram, is reincarnated as Maya Alejandra Sastry, niece of Lamb.

Kusa, son of Lord Ram is reincarnated as Nick Krishna Sastry, nephew of Lamb and also Noah.

Chandraketu, second son of Lakshmana is reborn as Lianna Isabel Sastry.

Karuna, step-brother of Pandava brothers is reincarnated as Varun Krovi, cousin of Lamb.

The four elder brothers of the Kalki avatar are Raman Akella, Ram Akella, and Bala Akella and Craig Davis.

Sri Govindaraja, brother of Lord Venkateshwara is reincarnated as Vinay Krovi.

Bhakta Prahlad is reincarnated as Nishith Acharya.

Maharishi Sootha is reincarnated as Durvasula Satya Narayana Murthy!

Sage Agustira is reincarnated as K. R. Venugopal, IAS retd.

Sage Valmiki is reincarnated as J. Harinarayan, IAS.

Sage Durvasa Maharishi and Parashurama was reincarnated as D. V. Subba Rao.

Lord Subbarmayam/Karthik is Vinay Prasad Durvasula.

Lord Veera Bhadra Swamy, a creation of and representative of Lord Shiva was reincarnated as Hota Veera Bhadra Rao, maternal great-grandfather.

Lord Dakshina Murthy was reincarnated as Durvasula Venkata Sastry, paternal great-grandfather.

Ishan Kolluri is Angada, the son of Laxman.

CHAPTER 8

Heroes

After Phil Bronstein wrote an exclusive in the San Francisco Chronicle that a local Navy Seal Team Six veteran who was the one who killed Osama Bin Laden could not find work and in Silicon Valley or anywhere and Rachel Maddow reported that Seth Moulton a war hero won his congressional race when a local paper reported that he was a decorated war hero but never bragged about it or mentioned it, my dad asked me a question!

He asked while watching television regarding Rep. Seth Moulton if I had done something like this without telling anyone and I nodded in affirmation I was the first Navy Seal Team Six member to shoot and kill Osama bin Laden. After all I ordered his hit on a United Airlines flight to San Francisco sitting next to an Air Marshal!

I was also the American POW in Vietnam who was being tortured, Sen. Jeremiah Denton, from Mobile, Alabama, who blinked Morse code back to Washington and the Pentagon that POW's of the USA were being tortured in the Hanoi Hilton.

Also, Osama went at me because I bought sandals at the World Trade Center with my cousin and a female friend. He thought that was a war against civilizations. Sandals are a secret between Jesus Christ and John the Baptist! I was also an Idol worshipping Hindu, a double thorn in his side.

When the Ten Commandments in Judaism were preached and taught by Moses and reiterated by Jesus Christ and Idol worship was prohibited, these messengers of God were referring to Greek Gods and Greek Idol worship and Greek Polytheism such as worship of ZEUS and PROMETHEUS etc. They were referring to Greek Mythology-related idol worship and not Hindu IDOL worship. They did not know much about Hinduism at that time and were not referring to Hindus, who of course, existed at the time. Hinduism is the world's oldest form of organized religion. Lord Shiva Temples existed even in the Middle East, Europe and Egypt at one time but were destroyed by Muslim, Christian, or Nomadic groups. Some are still in existence and studied and carbon dated by Archaeologists. There is also evidence of knowledge and study of the Lord Siva Temples in Africa and the ancient Middle East.

Every ancient culture including pagan cultures and indigenous people & the Abrahamic lineage religions, and world oldest organized religion of Sanatana Dharma (aka Hinduism/Vedic order) and offshoots of Hinduism refer to Their God as the Sun God, Sun King, the Light, the illumination, or Sun as creator of the Universe as in Bhagavad Gita and the Bible says Jesus is the Light and the Lamb is the Sun! The Ramayana states that Lord Ram and his father King Dasharatha are of the Suryavansham dynasty or Solar Dynasty.

In the Bible it states the Lamb and Son of Manu and Second Coming of Christ will be named "Word of God" (Revelation 19:13 NIV).

My Father for some reason insisted that I be named "Dinesh" which is not common for Telugu Indians. Dinesh means "din or day" and "Esh or Lord" meaning Day Lord or Sun God! The most famous mantra of Hindus is the Gayatri Mantri or Sandhyavandanam meaning chant for Illumination, light, and Worship of and blessings of the Sun!

My last name that my Dad gave me is "Sastry" which means Word of God as prophesied in the Bible. In Telugu India, the Family name is mentioned first and the First name "Sastry" is given as last name!

So, if my Dad as an educated man as he advised his brothers to do had listed his First name in the USA as Sastry and his last name as Durvasula as it should be, then I would be Dinesh Durvasula. Thus, my name would not be Word of God according to the bible.

My uncle Vedantam went by Vedantam Durvasula (named after Vedas) and my uncle Prasad went by Vinay Prasad Durvasula (named after Lord Vinayaka and Prasadam-offerings to God.) My Uncle Chanti stayed in India so he remained as Durvasula Satyanarayana Murthy (named after the Lord Satyanarayana or the East Godavari Zilla God) like Godzilla.

The two sisters are Annapurna and Suryamala named after Goddesses.

However, My Dad knew something that few people knew. Anyone who worked at United Airlines knows he said "Jesus Christ" every ten minutes when he is telling a joke, getting angry, or just expressing amazement.

You also know in the Bible Jesus is often referred to as Christ, Jesus. Name Backwards.

The family Name Durvasula is linked to Durvasa Mahamuni, the angry and powerful incarnation of Lord Shiva who was father of the Pandavas of the Mahabharat epic! Durvasula is also interchangeable with King David of Jewish scriptures. Durvasula came to the Middle East in the form David or Dawoud for a different set of people. The City of David is Jerusalem and the City of Durvasula/David is Peddapuram, EGDT, AP India and San Francisco, CA, USA!

My father's name was Durvasula V. Sastry or D. V. Sastry and my Grandfather's name was Durvasula V. Subbarao or D. V. Subbarao, both very close to "David", "Devudu", "Dvesham", and "Devi", "Devatha" and "DVD"! Also "Devastation", "Divisive", "Deviancy", Devastating", and "Disaster", "Desastre", "Dhavid", and "Destiny" "Stare Decisis, and "Dissaray" "Dynasty", "Delightful", and "Diversity", "Divine", "Device, "Disney", "Disease", "Statistics", "Stats," "Strategy", "Democracy", "Democratic Party", "Davos", "Danish Pastry" (bread/flesh of Christ)", "Salt or Salty of the Earth,", "Dish Network", "Mystery,", "Dysfunctional", "Diva", "Dissatisfy", "Istadevatha", " Distu, "Denise", "Dennis", "Don", "Dan", "Amnesty,", "Denies", "Dino Valentino who I was named after and also Dino the Dinosaur!, "DNA", "Vitamin D", "Diminish", "Diminutive", "Dense", "Douche", "Dick", "Diversion" "dissipated,"disillusion", "Denouement", "DeGeneres", "Distraction".

Thus, I am the root or descendant of "Durvasula" or "David" even though not apparent by my name. You must check the lineage and heritage.

I am also the Lion from the Tribe of Judah as David and Jesus and John the Baptist and Ram are from Judea!

Also, Ram is the son of Hezron and descendant of David in the Old Testament. Ram is also a male Lamb (another name for Son of Man) in Bible. Lord Ram in Hinduism is also the first human Incarnation of God or Son of Manu or the Alpha as Hinduism is the first organized religion in the world. This also explains Ramallah in Mideast and Ramzan or Ramadan in Islam. It also explains the fable Alladin like Allah-Din. The Kalki Avatar/Second Coming is the Omega!

Also, in his message to the Churches in Philadelphia, Jesus implies he will reveal "my new name!" (Revelation 22: 4 NIV)

CHAPTER 9
Messages

"And to the angel of the church in Philadelphia write: 'The words of the holy one, the true one, who has the key of David, who opens, and no one will shut, who shuts and no one opens.' I know your works. Behold, I have set before you an open door, which no one is able to shut. I know that you have but little power, and yet you have kept my word and have not denied my name. Behold, I will make those of the synagogue of Satan who say that they are Jews and are not, but lie—behold, I will make them come and bow down before your feet, and they will learn that I have loved you. Because you have kept my word about patient endurance, I will keep you from the hour of trial that is coming on the whole world, to try those who dwell on the earth. I am coming soon. Hold fast what you have, so that no one may seize your crown. The one who conquers, I will make him a pillar in the temple of my God. Never shall he go out of it, and I will write on him the name of my God, and the name of the city of my God, the new Jerusalem, which comes down from my God out of heaven, and my own new name. He who has an ear, let him hear what the Spirit says to the churches.'"

Revelation 3:7-13 ESVhttp://bible.com/59/rev.3.7-13.esv

I am coming soon to all of you! Be patient!

""I, Jesus, have sent my angel to testify to you about these things for the churches. I am the root and the descendant of David, the bright morning star." The Spirit and the Bride say, "Come." And let the one who hears say, "Come." And let the one who is thirsty come; let the one who desires take the water of life without price. I warn everyone who hears the words of the prophecy of this book: if anyone adds to them, God will add to him the plagues described in this book, and if anyone takes away from the words of the book of this prophecy, God will take away his share in the tree of life and in the holy city, which are described in this book. He who testifies to these things says, "Surely I am coming soon." Amen. Come, Lord Jesus! The grace of the Lord Jesus be with all. Amen."

Revelation 22:16-21 NIV

"Then I saw heaven opened, and behold, a white horse! The one sitting on it is called Faithful and True, and in righteousness he judges and makes war. His eyes are like a flame of fire, and on his head are many diadems, and he has a name written that no one knows but himself. He is clothed in a robe dipped in blood, and the name by which he is called is The Word of God. And the armies of heaven, arrayed in fine linen, white and pure, were following him on white horses. From his mouth comes a sharp sword with which to strike down the nations, and he will rule them with a rod of iron. He will tread the winepress of the fury of the wrath of God the Almighty. On his robe and on his thigh, he has a name written, King of kings and Lord of lords."

Revelation 19:11-16 ESVhttp://bible.com/59/rev.19.11-16.esv

Vedas in Europe. However, the Hindu religion was not a particular target of the Jews nor the Christians at the time of Jesus Christ and the apostles as it was not prevalent. Also, it will be proved that these Hindu idols are able the breath, see, hear, walk, and talk. You should also not idolize celebrity or humans more than God.

CHAPTER 10

The Mark of the Beast

The Mark of the Beast is the worship of the unfettered or unbridled free market forces. Many scholars call this the "invisible hand" (Adam Smith, The Labor of Nations) of unbridled or unfettered market forces. Ironically, President George W. Bush referred to the "invisible hand of God (that) guides the affairs of our nation". Thus the "invisible hand" has been used in the context of God's work on Earth and the unbridled or unfettered free market forces that guide the economy and personal and collective decision making. You should not worship the unbridled or unfettered free market forces above God, as this would be akin to worshipping money or making money your master. You cannot have two masters both money and God. Ironically, however, the Lamb/Son of Man is the Master and thus the primary market maker in the free market. He owns the major wealth and the major corporations. Thus, God covers all bases. God controls the affairs of this nation and also the "free" market. This is a very important point and takes a mind of wisdom to completely absorb. God is both manipulating and protecting the people from their own weaknesses.

Cost Benefit Analysis and Mark of the Beast

The American public, including many conservatives and hawks, have turned souron the Iraq war effort and certain foreign policy and economic initiatives of the government though it all initially "tasted like honey in their mouths" (Ezekiel 3:3 NIV) because they are intellectually believers in the free market theory and market-based decision making. They are subconsciously internalizing the cost benefit analysis (of Justice Learned Hand-similar to 'risk-rewards analysis') and coming to the conclusion that the emotional, physical, and monetary **COSTS** of the Iraq war and some foreign policy initiatives are greater than the supposed **BENEFITS** of the Iraq war and certain foreign policy and economic initiatives.

The State of Israel was secretly formed by God, D. V. Subba Rao, Clark Gifford, Prime Minister Winston Churchill, and of course, President Harry Truman.

We urge the Bush administration to help create a Palestinian State.

Synchronicity and Coincidence explain why there seems to be more than one answer to every riddle and symbol in the mystery of God and revelations and prophecies. If you miss one sign, you will get a chance to catch the next sign, and you know that something special and extraordinary is happening,

Ram/Shiva or Ramalingam is the Lion from the Tribe of Judah with the key to the scroll. Muslims have Ramallah and celebrate Ramadan and Ramzan. Jews have Ram's horn, and Ramstein, and Ram the son of Hezron and grandson of Judah. The Christians have the Lamb who is also a Ram. Hindus have Ram, the first and the last, son of Svayambhuva Manu (Son of Man) and also Shiva, who combined with Ram is Ramalingam. God and the Lamb each have Shiva Lingams which can give eternal life by supplying living water of Life or divine semen of life from Lord Shiva.

CHAPTER 11
Mystery Babylon/Kali Era

Despite coincidence and synchronicity, Durvasula Sastry, Lakshmi Sastry, and Dinesh Subbaraya Sastry (the Lamb/Son of Man) are not Mystery Babylon or the Prostitute on the city of 7 Hills. Thus, the silent harassment by car drivers who are actually government agents should end towards D. V. Sastry. Other subtle forms of harassment or war or distress should also end. We are not Mystery Babylon or the Prostitute and D. V. Sastry is not either of these things. We are also not equipped to accept or handle excessive abuse in this regard. The U. S. Government lied about these facts and made war, but the Lamb has won because he is the King of Kings and the Lord of Lords.

Mystery Babylon is the United States of America and its neoconservative government and political system and results of the political processes etc. In order to share or distribute the title of Mystery Babylon and Prostitute among the two major political parties and not blame just one, President Bush and Vice President Dick Cheney, Condoleezza Rice and Mayor Rudy Giuliani and Sen. Larry Craig among others are playing the role of Beast from the Earth and also Mystery Babylon and Prostitute but also sharing these roles partially with President Bill Clinton and two females, Speaker Nancy Pelosi and Senator Hillary Clinton, Madeleine Albright among others. Females are necessary as many biblical purists require that the prostitute be a female. I hope everyone understands this complexity. Other countries are also playing the Role of Mystery Babylon, which is actually the "Kali Yuga" or "Kali Era" being personified by Goddess Kali in the forms of various governments, political and governmental actors including Benazir Bhutto and General Musharraf of Pakistan (formerly pre-partitioned India), and women in entertainment etc. These powerful people and institutions are equipped to handle the scrutiny, derision, and harassment.

Think about all of this wisely. Remember that Oil dependency, Drug companies, and the Military Industrial Complex are part of Mystery Babylon. The Kali Era manifests in different individuals and institutions and behavior and is also referred to as Jezebel. While it is written that Jezebel leads followers into "sexual immorality" and "eating of sacrificed foods" (Acts 15:29 NIV) this could mean actual sexual immorality but more often means adulteries of faith by individuals who are consumed by the institutions and characteristics of the Kali Era/Yuga and Jezebel is another name for Kali and the Era she represents. **God expects Fidelity from the children of God to the word of God and departures from the teachings of God are adulteries.**

Many people instantly recognize the Statue of Liberty and New York City as Mystery Babylon, the City that rules the earth, and also the Prostitute. However, there is more complexity to this, so this is not the obvious answer but part of the complex answer. The French secret societies gave the Statue of Liberty as a gift to the USA to represent Mystery Babylon. The poem of Lazarus about the Wretched & the Poor reference the Church of Laodicea in the Biblical Book of Revelation!

When adulterous men who may be linked to Mystery Babylon appear in their press conferences (Clinton, Vitter, Craig, Spitzer, Kobe Bryant, Magic Johnson etc.) they appear with their wife because their wife is part of Mystery Babylon and says figuratively "I stand as Queen, I am not a widow, I do not mourn" (Revelation 18:7 NIV). This has become the practice. It is both an apology and an act of defiance and reinforcement.

The TRIUMPHAL ENTRY-- The Seventh King will come riding on a Donkey (Democrat) and perhaps Gently (depending on whether the Beast and False Prophet are captured.) The Seventh King will definitely come riding on a Donkey/Democrat.

Why the Lamb/Son of Man is a Democratic Party member:

As one former Reagan administration official humorously stated, "If Jesus Christ were to come back, liberals would put him in REHAB."

The Lamb/Son of Man is not addicted to alcohol, caffeine or nicotine. The Lamb/Son of Man has stopped smoking, and only started as the signal that where was some type of conspiracy with D. V. Subba Rao involved as cigarette smoke was his symbol. It was also a signal to a world-wide network that Subba Rao was alive and well and that the Son of Man/Lamb was in control of things. The Lamb put the cigarette in his mouth on Dec. 23, 2004, on his way to New Orleans as an international signal. Upon reaching New Orleans, there was a snowstorm for Christmas for the first time. The next day after Christmas, there was a Tsunami and Earthquake. All loyalists to God and the Lamb in the world and all angels in Heaven knew that the Lamb/son of Man was in charge with D. V. Subba Rao, God, because of the Cigarette in the mouth. Thus, the response to these events was proper. The Lamb/son of Man, Subba Rao, and Lord Hanuman had decided to attack the old Kingdom of Lord Rama as a message.

Jesus said, "The son of Man comes eating and drinking and you call him a drunkard" (Luke 7:34 NIV). Jesus also said, "All of these must happen" (Luke 21:9 NIV), and "no one may take away words from this book (Revelations 22:19 NIV)". The book is "Book of Revelations" and the New Testament, though to create belief before the judging of the dead and resurrection, many Old Testament prophecies and Vishnu Purana prophecies are coming true also. Thus, the Son of Man has stopped drinking for one week or months without withdrawal symptoms or negative effects, but the Son of Man must come "drinking "and must be called a "drunkard" as stated in the New Testament (Luke 7:34 NIV), otherwise there will be NO HEAVEN on EARTH and NO RESURRECTION. There is a wing of the Republican party that takes these words seriously, while most Democrats would not. Republicans have kept the topic of God in the national dialog just as similar conservative parties or groups have done in other countries. Thus, the Republicans have understood the Son of Man's dilemma and have decided, they will not worry about the behavior of the Son of Man as long as prophecies are fulfilled, and he has the mouth of a lion, eyes of blazing fire, etc.

However, the Democratic Party celebrates diversity and encourages helping the least of these and attempts to help the poor. The Democratic Party has made the Lamb/Son of Man, an Indian Hindu, feel comfortable in his native land, the United States of America. Democrats tend to let God judge others, execute others, and pass various judgements on others. Some Republicans feel that they should judge others as gatekeepers of the Kingdom of God. The Democrats did not assume they knew how to do this, and which religion was supreme and when to pass judgement on others.

It is obvious form the Senator Larry Craig case, that when it comes to the Living God, even Republicans want the Living God (an Indian Hindu) to actually be a progressive Democrat. The same dynamic holds true in other countries, particularly Democracies. Thus Jesus "comes riding on a Donkey (Zechariah 9:9 NIV)."

The Lamb/Son of Man will probably allow these men coordinate (with other prophets and Saints including women) the distribution of some wealth to the poor and middle class of the world as these leaders have worked hard for a long time on poverty-related and upward mobility issues.

The Beast from the Sea is the Reagan/Bush administration and to some observers the Bush/Cheney first term. It is Now the Trump Administration.

The Beast form the Earth is the Bush/Cheney administration, particularly the Bush/Cheney second term.it is now Vladimir Putin administration.

The Dragon, Serpent/Devil/Satan is contained within Kalit Devi/ Saturn Forces and manifests in various institutions, governments, and individuals Such as Putin and Russia, China and authoritarian Communism.

Wars in Kalki and Vishnu Puranas:

As stated before, the Kalki Puranas are satisfied by two Gods, including the marriage prophecies and the wars against Buddhists and Meat-eaters. D. V. Subba Rao, God, decided that Buddhists were the Japanese during WW II and meat-eaters were the Germans at the same time. Subba Rao, through Clark Gifford and others, called for the State of Israel to be created in order to fulfill prophecy by President Truman and Winston Churchill. Subba Rao approved of the use of Atom Bomb and sent such messages explicitly. Subba Rao even introduced the routine of buttermilk drinking by President Truman. The Wars against Buddhists and strange meat-eaters in Korea and Vietnam were also approved as prophesied.

Of course, Great Britain (a beast) made war against D. V. Subba Rao throughout his youth, but he overcame them as King of Kings and Lord of Lords at that time, and with him were faithful followers Mahatma Gandhi, Bhagat Singh, Sardar Vallabhai Patel, and other freedom-fighters.

The Robert S. Mueller investigation has several indictments of Russians who tries to interfere in USA elections to Help President Donald Trump. The Mueller report also details contacts between the Russians, let by Vladimir Putin and the Trump campaign. This leads one to conclude that the Trump administration was put into power by the Dragon, in Russia and not God as President Obama had been.

If fact when the Trump administration began separation children at the Texas border from their Mothers, this became more like a Dragon attacking a mother. The Obama Administration had a similar plan but was put into power by God.

The 2000 recount election between Vice President Al Gore and President George W. Bush also appeared to be an election where the government was empowered by the Dragon in some way.

Ultimately if Trump and Pence resign it will repeat the Nixon areas.

CHAPTER 12
Rumors of War

As many people have guessed, talk of a USA war with Iran is a "Rumor of War" (Matthew 24:6 NIV) and will not materialize. There will be rumors of wars, these things must happen, but everything will be okay. Nation will not rise against nation, as this already happened during the time of D. V. Subba Rao and World War II. There will be armies circling Jerusalem, but that is also okay. There will be an Israeli state and Palestinian state also. Iran is not a threat to world peace; the leadership of that country is in consonance with intelligence agencies' goals. Iran is like an eight King as the American CIA plays a strong role in that country.

Catholicism:

The Catholic Saint Anthony/Antonio is reincarnated as Mayor Joe Alioto.
The Catholic Saint Charles/Carlos is reincarnated as Gov. Bill Richardson.
The Catholic Saint Francis de Assisi is reincarnated as Late Mayor George Moscone.
The Catholic Saint Patrick is reincarnated as Rep. Patrick Kennedy, Son of Sen. Edward M. Kennedy.

Resurrection & Reincarnation:

Reincarnation ended officially in 1911 when D. V. Subba Rao was born as all souls were then prepared for the Resurrection and Judgement Day. However, extraordinary individuals who may pique the interests of the Lamb and God such as George Washington, King Akbar and Jodhaa,

Abraham Lincoln, Frederick Douglas, Harriet Tubman, Thomas Jefferson, Chandragupta Maurya, Alexander the Great, and Chanakya and many slaves were given salvation/Moksha and thus freed from reincarnation as their souls were preserved for Resurrection.

The Resurrection will be in flesh and blood and of the soul, so buried bodies and cremated bodies will both be resurrected in full, healthy form. The Resurrected will have access to practical and tangible accessories and necessities. The Oceans will be partially eliminated and in place lost civilizations and land will appear, housing some of the resurrected dead.

The Dead are currently in white robes and awaiting the Resurrection with full knowledge of what is happening now on Earth and of the Lamb/Son of Man's teachings and activities. Others have been killed in name only and are actually alive to join the resurrection. This was done to fulfill prophecies and ensure that those awaiting a resurrection will have something tangible to look forward to without disappointment.

Credit Rating/Score deception:

In keeping with them that worship of unbridled or unfettered free markets capitalism or free markets in general is taking the Mark of the Beast, one number of the Beast is the Credit Score. Theoretically, no person may buy large items without a Credit Rating Score of 666 or higher. This also affects selling of Real Estate in a down market. The Lamb/Son of Man despises the credit bureau system as it is riddled with inaccuracies and iniquities. Similarly, many people do not buy or sell without use of credit or debit cards. Many consider the spending EARMARKS by U. S. Congress and the President of the USA, Especially President George W. Bush, to be Marks of the BEAST as no one can buy or sell without being affected by the EARMARKS.

Does 9/11/01 calculate from 666? It does if you calculate Boeing 777, Boeing 767, Boeing

Rider on the Black Horse:

The Rider on the Black Horse with Scales in his hands is Gov. Edmund G. "Jerry" Brown, Jr, who is now Attorney General of California. Vice President Al Gore is another rider on a black horse. They have both literally said "Come!" many times and offered Beers and wine at their homes to the Lamb/Son of Manu.

The Lamb went to his destruction and was Pierced and Slain and 3 AM Phone Call:

The Lamb was indeed pierced and Slain (Luke 9:22, Rev. 5:12, and Rev. 5:6 NIV) by government agents on September 26, 2003 at about 1:00 A. M. at a night club in Washington, DC while he was with businesspeople from California and the Middle East. The Lamb was involved in various business functions that day with a financial firm and was meeting with many prominent persons. In a movie: "Vanilla Sky" type of moment, the Lamb joked with two different persons, that it was the best day of his life as several important deals were being completed and new deals were starting. Subsequently, government agents ambushed the Lamb in a bathroom and hit him in the head with a hammer. The agents concocted a story and tried to make the incident look like a brawl or fight. The Lamb was in a blue suit or **"vestige or robes that were completely dripping or soaked in blood." (Revelation 19:13) The business card of the Lamb with his name was in his right pocket at his thigh and in the front pocket of his coat. The Lamb also had a mobile phone in the right pocket, at his right thigh with him name on the welcome screen.**

The Lamb was slain and pierced and went to his destruction. The covert operatives who work most clubs on the street frequented by the Lamb, immediately went into action to protect the image of the Lamb but cover up the incident. They did not allow the businesspeople to see what happened. The government agents from another agency who committed the act of war against the Lamb calculated that one of the businesspeople could claim the body that early morning and quietly cover up the incident and inform the family of the Death of the Lamb.

A stunned spy who is actually a famous actress and singer, cleared the blood from the crime scene and a she with help put the body in an alley outside of the club. The dead Lamb then came back to life, as agents watched, and hailed a cab and lay in the cab dripping in blood. The Lamb directed the taxi driver home and not to the hospital and even directed the taxi without sitting up or looking and while in semi-conscious state. The Lamb then went home slept in the bloody robes and then washed the suit and shirt the next day. The Lamb woke up at 6:30 A. M. and called a colleague from the night before and informed him that he could not attend a Venture Capitalist meeting due to disfigured face. The maid of the Lamb, also a spy, then cleaned the blood in the bedroom.

The Lamb paid the taxi driver for stains and return of his cell phone. Friends urged the Lamb/Son of Man to contact police and see doctors. The Lamb waited a few days, healed himself and then went to doctors who found slight damage to the nose and lip area, but no head injuries or brain damage. They had no idea that the Lamb had died, was hit by a hammer, and then resurrected himself. However, many world leaders and former world leaders were briefed immediately that the Lamb/Son of Man lay in robes dripping with blood with his name at his thigh and also that the Lamb had gone to destruction and come back to life. The world leaders were astonished, and this began an intensified war against the Lamb and his business and career activities.

Thus, very few people know that the Lamb died and came back to life and covered-up the incident.

This is a very important fact. It is very rare in the history of the world that some living entity has died and come back to life almost immediately. The Lamb had done nothing wrong that night and was not inebriated. Like most allegations against the Lamb, a false story was concocted.

Many prominent United States leaders and former leaders and national security agencies were briefed of the incidents in systematic ways. Briefings were conducted both in-person and by phone. The CCTV video was also passed around.

Song to World:
"Diamonds and Pearls" Artist Prince

Photo Gallery

President Clinton and Dinesh Sastry in Washington, DC in 1995

Durvasula Sastry with Gov. Jerry Brown in San Francisco

(Back Row) Manoj Sastry, Lakshmi Sastry, DV Sastry, Dinesh
(Front Row) Nicholas Krishna Sastry, Lianna
Isabel Sastry, Maya Alejandra Sastry

Vice President Gore, Second Lady Tipper Gore, Dinesh, First
Lady Hillary Clinton, President Clinton in 2000.

First Lady Clinton and Dinesh in US Embassy in New Delhi, India in 1995.

DV Subbarao and Durvasula Atchuthamba (Grandparents)

Dinesh, Manoj, Alejandra Espinosa Sastry, Lakshmi, and DV Sastry

(Back Row) Manoj, Ally, Lakshmi, DV Sastry, Dinesh
(Front Row) Lianna, Maya, Nicky

Prime Minister P. V. Narasimha Rao of India at
United Nations, New York City and Dinesh.

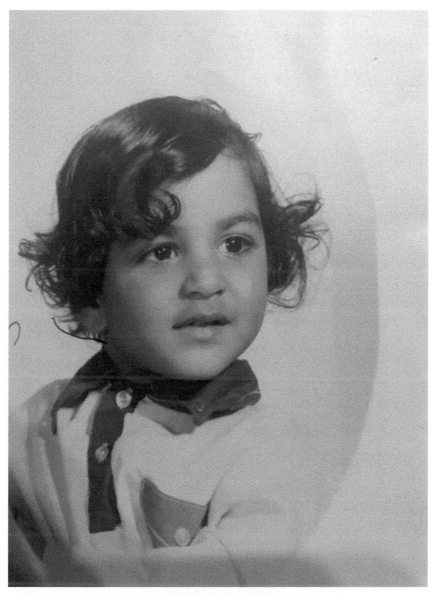

Dinesh's baby picture

Prime Minister Atal Behari Vajpayee in New Delhi, India and Dinesh.

Deputy Prime Minister L. K. Advani in New Delhi, India and Dinesh

Lord Krishna guides Arjuna in Chariot while reciting the Bhagavad Gita

The Shiva Linga (Phallic symbol)

Fourteen Hindu Goddesses

Lakshman, Lord Ram, Goddess Sita, Lord Hanuman
(Monkey God who is kneeling)

Lord Ganesha (the Elephant God)

Jilted & Scorned Goddess Kali dances on Lord Shiva
whose clothing resembles a Leopard

Scarlet & Purple Kali Tramples on Lord Shiva who
is a beast that resembles a Leopard.

Goddess Durga on a Tiger.

Jesus Christ is the Light or the Sun.

Lord Krishna plays flute with his female friends.

Lord Shiva meditates on Mount Kailas in the Himalayas.

CHAPTER 13

Lamb's Job Description:

The Lamb will be King of Kings and Lord of Lords and thus ultimately oversee the probity and effectiveness of world Governance, Public Policy Making, and the play a major role in the Global Planning Council by deciding what problems will be solved by divine/supernatural solutions and intervention. The Lamb will the titular head of all world armies and militaries and establish, administer, and oversee the tradition of War games and military exercises between nations. Comity between nations will be celebrated and enmity and animosity between nations will be abolished.

As the Lamb/Son of Man has and will have even more extraordinary multitasking capabilities, the Lamb will serve many corporations/businesses at the Chairman/CEO level including the those in sectors such as Media/ Entertainment, Fashion, Banking/Finance, and Technology and perhaps be involved in even the Auto, Chemical, Oil, Energy, and Telecom sectors. In order to maintain his status as the primary market maker in a global, hybrid economy that is based on a revised form of market-based capitalism, the Lamb/Son of man/Master will maintain majority ownership in various corporations and financial institutions. The Lamb will directly or indirectly determine the appropriate Price/Earnings ratio for a given public equity without encouraging unnecessary and unjustified inflationary pressure. There will be quality-based competition instead of only bottom-line-based competition with best business practices often being incorporated within this same context but NOT at the expense of communities, jobs, workers benefit and wages. There could be a move away from quarterly earnings reports to biannual and annual reports in order to curb volatility in markets and encourage long range planning by corporations.

There will be an international version of the Central Bank and an international Federal Reserve Board as well as sister member boards within the various members of the global confederacy of partially independent Nations. The Lamb will sit on these boards or at least abide by the advice of these boards but in the end-use divine methods to ensure that fiscal and monetary policy is optimum and equitable and successful. Both Dr. Alan Greenspan and Dr. Laura D'Andrea Tyson, Dr. Y. V. Reddy IAS, Dr. Duvurri Subba Rao IAS, and Dr. Ben Bernanke will find a place on these international boards.

The Lamb/Son of Man will administer a type of National Security/Asset Tax (coined by Economist Ravi Batra of Texas) as national security will be provided by the Lamb and God and those who have accumulated enormous net assets have the most to lose with threats to the border, the security, or the integrity of a nation. A net asset tax is difficult to administer because of manipulations by accountants, and lawyers, and because of cheating. However, the Lamb and his angels will administer an asset tax without being susceptible to cheating or manipulation by use of divine powers. Income tax will eventually be phased out of the global tax regimes.

Thus, the financial market, now known as the "free" market, will function appropriately, but it will be a clear and transparent fact that God and the Lamb are the Masters of the market and Masters of the Universe. You cannot serve two masters, both money and God, and thus the market will have only one master.

The Lamb will also resurrect the dead and provide eternal life to many. He will also heal the sick, the blind, the deaf, the dumb, the physically challenged, the mentally challenged, the chemically dependent, and others in pain. The Lamb and God will also help reverse ageing to some extent in the elderly and the Lamb will allow many elder people to rejuvenate themselves by freeing them from curses of old age such as frailty arthritis, balding, and loss of sexual appetite and function. There shall be no more curse on humans and thus women will not have the inconvenient cramps and bleeding and other curses during their menstrual cycles.

The Lamb will perform most duties of creation and destruction on Earth. The Lamb and God will receive feedback from followers, prophets, Saints, and servants in order to maintain the proper quality of human life including the education, and other socioeconomic and quality of life measures.

CHAPTER 14

Consequences of New World and Heaven on Earth:

The Lamb/Son of Man spends a great deal of time and thought on and with the Politicians, public servants, Media elite and opinion-makers, the ambitious, and sometimes even the idealistic. These are the people that will require the most adjustment in the Kingdom of God and slightly adjusted notion of what is right and wrong and efficient or appropriate.

The majority of working families, students, entrepreneurs, or business executives will find the Kingdom of God to be an ideal paradise and very happy that the world is heading toward a Utopian state. However, the political elite, the most ambitious, and the public servants in the long run, will have to adjust certain ideals of what it is ultimate success and what is an ideal system of governance, economy and the like. Life will not be a zero-sum game. As the Lamb and God solve many serious problems with the help of divine powers and angels with superhuman powers, the public servants will feel a void that must be filled by exploration of new lands, newly resurrected historical personalities, and the idea that the Lamb and God will always be the ultimate authority and God will rule permanently on Earth. Human leaders, those with the calling to do great things, will have much to do but should also realize that the great improvements and debates about improvements will eventually be on the margins of perfection, and work toward a more perfect and just and heavenly world.

Who does the jobs that the wealthy or even the middle class do not want to do?

The question of who will do the jobs that were once done by the poor and middle class is important in a world that moves toward zero poverty rate and a better quality of life. The jobs once done by the poor and middle class but now finding a shortage of workers will be done by the Lamb/Son of Man's own angels who are not human.

Who can the wealthy look down upon and ridicule or insult in a world without poverty?

This is not a necessary condition or attribute of Utopian society or Heaven and thus there will not be much effort put toward PRESERVING this luxury unless it is in the context of appropriate constructive criticism or satire and comedy.

What will happen to professions that thrive on problems or conflicts?

They will be reformed and then compensated. For example, the Lord of Lords will solve many of the problems now reserved for Doctors, Prosecutors, Police, and lawyers and politicians. However, these professions, including some like plastic surgery, dentistry, clergy or priests, and others that persons will move away from in order to seek more permanent and direct solutions from God and the Lamb, will be maintained and attended to so as to prevent massive dislocation or economic upheaval. This would include the Drug industry, the energy and oil industry, the military industrial complex and medical and law enforcement industries and agencies and even the world's military organizations and services.

What will happen to the residents of the small town in India that will suddenly become the "New Jerusalem" and expand into a type of nation-state?

The people of Peddapuram and nearby areas, many of them of modest means and skills will be give the proper and appropriate hard skills and soft skills including linguistic skills and etiquette according to their prayers and also given wealth and wardrobes commensurate with requirements of the New Jerusalem so that they will not feel intimidated, or intruded upon by visitors to the New Jerusalem. The transformation will occur in almost seamless fashion, and the people will not harbor resentment. Many of the resorts, hotels, and restaurants and other institutions in the New Jerusalem will be staffed and supplanted by the Lord's Angels who have superhuman capabilities. It will be amazing and take place according to the lifelong wishes of D. V. Subba Rao.

Abortion:

"Mother of Abominations" (Revelation 17:5 NIV) can refer to corruption, Wars, failed policies, and INJUSTICES. However, this phrase can also refer to abortions and surprise or unplanned children or pregnancies. Thus, as the Lamb/Son of Man supports the "Roe vs. Wade" disposition in the USA Supreme Court (and the legally constructed "Right to Privacy" that it guarantees), and has explained that the soul is added to fetus, thereby constituting life, only at the TIME of birth, and since the Lamb/Son of Man was a member of the Democratic Party leadership in the past, it can be extrapolated that one meaning for "ABOMINATIONS" is "unplanned pregnancies". However, no one should be pro-abortion or celebrate abortions.

Description of Kalki Avatar and His Supernatural Powers in Hindu scriptures:

The Mahabharata is more specific in its description of the Kalki-Avatar. On being asked by Yuddhistira, the sage, Markandeya, describes the Kalki Incarnation. He says that inspired by the Supreme Spirit, in a certain village called Shambal, a son will be born in the house of a Brahman named VISHNUYASHA and this boy's name shall be Kalki Vishnuyasha. This Brahman boy shall be an extremely powerful, intelligent and valiant personage. He shall get all weapons, armies, etc., at will. Collecting a huge army of Brahman warriors, he shall go about setting order of righteousness in the world. He shall not only re-establish the rule of dharma but shall also herald the advent of the Golden Age or the Satyayuga of the next cycle of time.

In [a] talk [with Sage Markandeya] a few years before the Kali Age began [and recorded in the Mahabharata], Lord Vishnu told how Light would come to earth when the evils of the [Kali] Age had reached a level that required the direct action of God. Lord Vishnu said to the sage Markendaya: "When evil is rampant upon this earth, I will take birth in the family of a virtuous man, and assume a human body to restore tranquility by the extermination of all evils; for the preservation of rectitude and morality, I will assume an inconceivable human form when the season for action comes. In the Kali Age of sin, I will assume an Avatar form that is dark in color. I will be born in a family in South India. This Avatar will possess great energy, great intelligence and great powers. Material objects needed for this Avatar's mission will be at his disposal as soon as He will think of them. He will be victorious with the strength of virtue. He will restore order and peace in the world. This Avatar will inaugurate a new Era of Truth and will be surrounded by spiritual people. He will roam over the earth adored by the spiritual people."

"The people of the earth will imitate this Avatar's conduct, and there will be prosperity and peace. Men will once more betake themselves to the practice of religious rites. Educational centers for the cultivation of Brahmic lore, and temples, will reappear again everywhere. Ashrams will be filled with men of Truth. Rulers of the earth will govern their kingdoms virtuously. The Avatar will have an illustrious reputation."

This prophecy concerning the Kalki Avatar, from the Mahabharata, is collaborated in the ancient classic, the Vishnu Purana, which also mentions that this Avatar will display great superhuman powers in establishing the new age of Truth. It adds that, "His parents will be devotees of Vishnu, and will reside in a village worshipping the cowherd form of Sri Krishna."

Why was Lamb/Son of Man (as was President George Bush) dancing and doing other such things a couple of years back?

To some extent, he was humbling himself like a child as in scriptures. However, the main reason he was dancing (though not in a serious or disciplined or skillful way) is because intelligence agencies and Hindus are looking for signs if the Lamb is Lord Shiva and Lord Shiva is known for dancing. Thus, the Lamb/Son of Man put on a dancing show at times. Other attributes and characteristics can be explained as well. Similarly, Lord Krishna was known for playing the Flute and singing.

Immaculate Conception and Fusion of Holy Trinity into Virgin Birth of Divine Soul:

On March 13, 1971 the Holy Trinity, Lord Brahma (the Holy Spirit), Lord Shiva (the Father), and Lord Vishnu (the Son) fused or merged into or created a Divine Soul that entered and was attached to the soul and fetus of Dinesh S. Sastry, the Lamb/Son of Man. This, in effect, was a form of Immaculate conception or Virgin Birth of the Divine Soul of the Savior.

Jesus Christ Crucified and the Lamb/Son of Man pierced and slain and targeted in War:

The Lamb/Son of Man and Jesus Christ suffered ridicule and crucifixion as a gift to the human race. Jesus suffered in ordered to save the human race from sins and the stringent rules or dharma set by God and Religion. The prevailing conditions for Hindus, Christian, Jews and Muslims to enter Heaven, receive true salvation, or enter the Kingdom of God place a very high standard for the human race in the collective or as individuals to adhere to, abide by, or satisfy. Thanks to Jesus Christ, D. V. Subba Rao and the Lamb/Son of Man were sent in order to change certain definitions of the proscriptions or limiting conditions for entry into Heaven. Additionally, all prophets and Saints such Moses and Abraham and the Counselor were created as imperfect souls or vessels with an eye toward absolving many from punishment for common weaknesses as these Prophets also had the same weaknesses. The Irony should not be lost on anyone. This is why Jesus Christ was crucified, otherwise no person would satisfy the Ten Commandments or Lord Krishna's Dharma as set out in the Bhagavad Gita.

Book of Life:

The Book of Life is written in the Leaves of the Nadi Shastras, that are leaves written by Sages according Lord's description of each human being's life.

Future of Vedas:

The Rig Vedas will remain relevant. The Soma Vedas will remain relevant. However, the Yajur Vedas will be less relevant in the Kingdom of God which is Heaven on Earth. This is because the Yajur Vedas advocate renunciation of worldly possessions, activities, and wants and the life of a sanyasi as a method and means to achieve salvation or moksha. However, when the Kingdom of God is Heaven on Earth and eternal life for the children of God, then this by definition is automatic moksha or salvation, and thus the Yajur Vedas are not so relevant.

The Spectrum of Color:

In the spectrum of color, Black is absence of any color, and white is the combination of all primary colors merged together. Thus, the robes of people will be made white in the blood of the Lamb. This is a figurative description and not a literal description.

Angels from Heaven:

The angels from Heaven that follow the Lamb/Son of Man and the Brahmin angels that follow the Kalki Avatar are not human and have some divine knowledge and powers and work in various intelligence agencies, hospitals, emergency medical services, militaries, police departments, law enforcement agencies, lawyers, doctors, and business people and even Mafia and gang members. They are everywhere and carry though God's orders and help fulfill God's words and prophecies. They are certainly in the FBI, CIA, KGB, U. S. Military, U. S. Secret Service, various American and Indian hospitals, the CBI in India, the RAW in India, and IB in India. They can read the mind of the Lamb/son of Man and also read the future and, thus, act without explicit orders, they also supply information that the Holy Spirit passes through them to the Lamb/Son of Man.

Why are Hindu Gods and Goddesses pictured with multiple arms and multiple heads?

The Gods can be divided between more than one person and appear in different forms; thus, they are depicted with multiple heads and arms.

Why do bad things happen to good people?

Prayers and rituals can help mitigate or assuage a bad period or bad karma and create good karma, but much of karma is predetermined by your fate and destiny and past life. Fate and destiny are the result of the positions of the planets and stars at the time of your birth. Karma factors in your fate and destiny with sins and good deeds of past life and present life. Prayer can affect karma to differing degrees depending on the individual souls and situation or circumstances. Many who die now are resting from their labors as they are dying in the Lamb//Son of Man/Kalki avatar and will be resurrected with a better life than before.

In the Kingdom of God most people will start with salvation or moksha, especially infants and small children, and will receive bad Karma as a result of evil deeds or sins. They will be judged by God and the Lamb/Son of Man and will not be burdened by horoscope, fate, destiny, or karma.

Why has the United States maintained porous borders?

The United States has for the past four decades maintained relatively porous borders and liberal immigration policy hoping that California, or New York or Washington, D. C. might become the New Jerusalem and the Kingdom of God. It is written that "the gates to the city will never be shut, day or night (Revelation 21:25 NIV)". This was taken to mean that the borders to the United States should not block immigrants if the USA wanted to become the New Jerusalem and the Kingdom of God.

CHAPTER 15
Marriage Bureau

The Lamb/Kalki/Son of Man will create a marriage bureau for close friends and family that uses different technologies and powers and future reading to connect brides and grooms with their lifetime soulmate. Admiration for the bureau and envy will cause the citizens of many nations and many ethnic backgrounds to demand access and coverage under such an "arranged marriage" bureau. The Lamb/Ram will originally make it available only to close friends and family as part of a master plan, and not force such a bureau on the people in a coercive or precipitous way.

Heaven Will Fit on Earth:
The Earth will retain many characteristics to promote continuity and fond memories and celebration of institutions and cultures. However, Heaven and the Resurrection will fit both in terms of space and emotions on Earth as the much of the SEAS and OCEANS will turn to land and uncover surprises.

As said before, the Kingdom of God will not be a fascist society, but be a nearly Utopian society with just the right amount of tension, surprise, unpredictability, diversity, and problems to keep talented people, including the Lamb/Son of Man and God busy enough to avoid complacency and retain proper stimulation of the senses.

The Holder of Keys to the Abyss and the Destroyer of Evils:
Lord Shiva lived in an Abyss or cave in Mt. Kailas of the Himalayas. Lord Shiva has the keys to the Abyss. Lord Shiva is the King and angel of

the Abyss. In Hebrew is referred to as Abaddon and in Greek he is referred to as Apollyon, meaning Destroyer etc.

The Utah Mine where the miners are trapped looks almost identically like the Abyss in which Lord Shiva has lived for generations.

Theory of Evolution and Creationism

If you study the Vishnu Purana, you will read that there are 10 official, predestined incarnation of Vishnu (Son of God) and perhaps several more because the eighth incarnation, Lord Krishna, stated in the Bhagavad Gita that he (or Son of God) would incarnate from time to time when it was necessary.

Lord Ram is the seventh incarnation of Vishnu and the first completely human and civilized incarnation.

There were six other incarnations of the son of God in subhuman forms such as micro-organisms and animals such as fish, reptile, amphibians, and mammals. Thus, God incarnated several times along the way in order to further the process of EVOLUTION, or theory of Evolution or Darwinism. Thus, there are merits in both the arguments for evolution and the arguments for CREATIONISM.

God is the catalyst or driving force in the theory of evolution and the furtherance of SCIENCE.

Do not destroy the Earth, as it is God's creation.

Deep Throat as Code Word

"Deep Throat" refers not any individual or persons but the secret that Lord Shiva is the key to all revelations and prophecies and is the "FATHER" and is also represented by his Phallic Symbol-The Shiva Lingam thought to represent male or cosmic energy. The Mt. Everest reference comes from the fact that Lord Shiva historically lived in a cave/abyss in the Himalayas mountains. You will get eternal life by eating and drinking the flesh and blood of the Lamb and God. However, this is actually mystical drink called soma (also called "Living water") and will be explained at the appropriate time so as not to confuse doctors and chemists now. It is true that the Shiva Lingams are the divine or mystical "Penis" of Lord Shiva.

This is why the descendants of Abraham call circumcision their covenant with God. Circumcision creates the appearance of the "Shiva Lingam" as the Shiva Lingam is rounded off at the top.

Thus "Deep Throat" refers to only Lord Shiva and also the fact that some vile humor and some innuendo by comedians about prophets and Saints and other servants will be allowed but blasphemy against the God and Lamb and their families will not be tolerated in the Kingdom of God, as it would subvert or undermine young people's faith who have not lived through these times or are too young to understand.

TIMETABLES FOR THE DAY OF THE LORD

The Republicans in a recent debate argued over timetables in IRAQ and for withdrawal of troops. The Lamb/Son of Man cannot announce a timetable for the Day of the Lord, the Resurrection, the ending of conflicts etc. As the scriptures say, "armies will surround Jerusalem" (Luke 21:20 NIV) but these things must happen as must "rumors of war" (Matthew 24:6 NIV) with Iran or other conflicts.

No one may know the hour or the day of the lord, not even the Angels from Heaven, but only the Father. The Father does become the son and the Son becomes the father, but this is an internal issue and not for public scrutiny. Also because of the various cycles of time that Buddha had explained, the Earth has been destroyed many times and re-created with the same actors repeatedly. However, this time, the World will not be destroyed completely and Heaven or the Kingdom of God will be on Earth and the Lamb and God will live forever on Earth with the children of God.

As the angels from Heaven have seen the cycles before, they know what will happen even before it happens. It is as if they are reading from an arranged guidebook or schedule of information or a "scroll". They will assist the intelligence agencies, world militaries, and world leaders in planning for the Day of the Lord and will know the day of the lord but not the precise hour. We must assiduously follow the scriptures and revelations as no word may be removed from them to prevent evil forces (the DEVIL or SATAN or Dragon) from arising again in one thousand years.

Please remember that the brides of the Lamb are young and many of the female followers of the Lamb are patiently waiting and have some precedent-setting age considerations. Similarly, the dead who are actually dead and those whose deaths have been fabricated are also patiently waiting for the Resurrection. Thus, we know the Day of the Lord is coming soon, perhaps before the coming of the Seventh King, that is the seventh elected President during the lifetime of the Lamb/Son of Man or the Seventh Elected Democratic President since first King-like modern, President FDR.

It is a fact that even President George W. Bush and the Republicans want to end the war and prevent more troops from dying but are concerned that "armies will surround Jerusalem (Luke 21:20 NIV)" and that prophecies must be fulfilled. The staff (angels) of the Lamb/Son of Man are not allowing General Petraeus or other leaders to end the war in Iraq yet. Similarly, Osama bin Laden will be captured in a timely fashion in order to fulfill prophecies and at that time, Al Qaeda, the Taliban, and Hamas and Hezbollah's will all surrender or be destroyed.

The two consecutive periods of 1260 days and 42 months began in December 2000. We are now going toward 1335 days but are certainly in End Times and at end of the Kali Era.

The United States of America and some leaders including President George W. Bush and General Jerry Brown will have the opportunity to announce or reveal the Lamb/Son of Man before commencing activities and the remainder of prophecies and Rapture. There could also be a ceremony for the King of Kings and Lord of Lords and the Existence of God, D. V. Subba Rao. All this will take place in the United States of America under the auspices of prophets and Saints.

War, Crime, Overpopulation, pollution, and traffic:
Just as the Lamb, God, and the CIA and network of angels can end Wars, many crimes, smuggling, and drug trafficking, and overpopulation in China and India (millions of robots without souls), they can also end road traffic in San Francisco/Bay Area, and Washington, DC and other places as much of it is generated by the angels.

U. S. A. agencies have been involved in Drug trafficking in Colombia, Nicaragua, Mexico, China, Afghanistan etc. through Pacifica, CA; Daly City, CA; and Los Angeles, CA etc., Miami, Fl; and New York, New York.

U. S. A. agencies have been involved in disease propagation and even creation of some strains of disease.

The Song of Moses is "**My Way**", by Frank Sinatra
Dr. M. L. King, Jr. and D. V. Subba Rao became great friends in the 1950s. D. V. Subba Rao collaborated with Dr. King on the "I Have a Dream" speech

and also advised Dr. King to create a "sea of white angels" in " white Nehru" caps. Durvasula Venkata Subba Rao wrote the first draft of the "I Have a Dream" Speech by Dr. Martin Luther King, Jr. and sent it by telex. He also advised that the meeting at the mall be a "sea of white" angels and suggested everyone should wear Nehru style white caps that were made famous by the Indian freedom struggle and Mahatma Gandhi.

Sen. Barack Obama gave a brilliant speech on MLK JR day. The Lamb/ Son of Man did not collaborate on this speech but was proud that Obama started the speech by mentioning Joshua and the walls of Jericho. By comparing Joshua to a civil rights leader, Obama is promoting the proper narrative that President Lyndon Johnson is the reincarnation of Joshua and President Kennedy is the reincarnation of Moses and Dr. Martin Luther King, Jr. is the reincarnation of JOB.

Similarly, Obama mentioned the Reagan coalition as an example of Unity in US politics as Reagan was the reincarnation of King Solomon.

Angels from Heaven

There are at least 72 Million angels from Heaven on Earth who serve the Lamb/son of Man. However, there are 10,000 times 10,000 and even up to 200,000,000 or slightly more angels that appear from time to time but can also disappear and do not have permanent jobs or even permanent roles. They could show up at bar fight to defend the Lamb for example.

Creation of God and Universe
A Supernatural Force created The Divine Sun who created Vishnu and Vishnu created the universe, Shiva, and Brahma. Vishnu is also Jesus Christ.

Bhagavad Gita Chapter 7 Verse 8
O son of Kunti, I am the taste of water, the light of the sun and the moon, the syllable om in the Vedic mantras; I am the sound in ether and ability in man.

Bhagavad Gita Chapter 4 Verse 6
Although I am unborn and My transcendental body never deteriorates, and although I am the Lord of all living entities, I still appear in every millennium in My original transcendental form.

Bhagavad Gita Chapter 4 Verse 4
Arjuna said: The sun-god Vivasvan is senior by birth to You. How am I to understand that in the beginning You instructed this science to him?

Bhagavad Gita Chapter 4 Verse 5
The Personality of Godhead said: Many, many births both you and I have passed. I can remember all of them, but you cannot, O subduer of the enemy, Arjuna

Bhagavad Gita Chapter 4 Verse 10
Being freed from attachment, fear and anger, being fully absorbed in Me and taking refuge in Me, many, many persons in the past became purified by knowledge of Me -- and thus they all attained transcendental love for Me.

Bhagavad Gita Chapter 4 Verse 9
One who knows the transcendental nature of My appearance and activities does not, upon leaving the body, take his birth again in this material world, but attains My eternal abode, O Arjuna.

Bhagavad Gita Chapter 4 Verse 8
To deliver the pious and to annihilate the miscreants, as well as to reestablish the principles of religion, I Myself appear, millennium after millennium.

Bhagavad Gita Chapter 4 Verse 7
Whenever and wherever there is a decline in religious practice, O descendant of Bharata, and a predominant rise of irreligion -- at that time I descend Myself.

CHAPTER 16
Creation of Divine Sun, God, and Universe

A supernatural force created the Sun and the Sun God created Lord Vishnu who then created Lord Brahma and Lord Shiva and the Universe! Then Lord brahma created the Vedas and first Human Being Svayambhuva Manu which is the origin of the words human and man! Lord Shiva destroyed the world with a flood and Manu saved all animals and human life in pairs! Lord Shiva destroyed the world because he found... it boring and homogenous with only Indians and Hindus! Lord Vishnu also granted Manu the status of always being the father of lord Vishnu when he descends to Earth! Vishnu also incarnated several times as sub human forms to further the process of evolution! ultimately humans were created in mass and Lord Shiva helped by incarnating as Lord Hanuman who was granted eternal life and still lives today and as a duplicate entity of Lord Shiva! he has allowed pillaging and conquering of India in the name of diversity at the urging of Lord Vishnu who loves different foods, different cultures, and different beautiful women! hanuman (A Monkey God, looks like Michael Jackson after his surgeries. Lord Shiva also came as Durvasa Maharishi who gave birth to the Pandavas, the cousins of Lord Krishna(Vishnu)!The world has gone through several cycles of creation and destruction as explained by Buddha(also Vishnu) in the Kalanchakra Tantra in Peddapuram, Ap, India, which can be monitored and proven by another planet in the universe called Vishnu Lok! In the most recent era, Lord Shiva gave the laws of God to Moses on Mt Kailas and Moses started Judaism with a bond with a sacred stone the Siva lingam which led to circumcision. Earlier Lord Brahma came as Abraham and Lord Shiva came as King David. Lord Shiva also created the Egyptian civilization!

Jesus Christ came in this era as a Jew and helped create more diversity around the world by asking for the good news to be preached around the world! He also talked about the Resurrection and eternal life! He was counseled by Hindu gurus in India! He told the whole world that the Messiah would be the Son Of Manu keeping with the Svayambhuva Manu boon as father if God! Svayambhuva Manu is also Lord Ganesha son of Lord Shiva! Guru Nanak was created to stop Hindus from being raped and forcefully converted by Muslim invaders! Hence the Sikh religion! Prophet Muhamned was created to create the concept that God is Great, Almighty, Omnipotent, and beef eating is allowed, and that women should not be as sexually promiscuous as men because they are receivers and can become Pregnant which is an honor (motherhood) and also a curse in some situations! In other words, they shouldn't be sluts! There will be celestial angels (-as Hillary Clinton said in 2008) in the Kingdom of a God to satisfy the Male sexual appetite. Many women in Bollywood and Hollywood and music and politics are pretending to be promiscuous to mimic the end times prophecies of end of the Kalki Yuga and Biblical Revelation 14:4 NIV where women are purchased from among many men and follow the king of kings and lord of lords around the world for eternity and are first fruits to The Lord like Lord Krishna's Gopikas and multiple wives and The same prophet who is John the Baptist is also Prophet Guru Nanak is also the Prophet Muhammed! The weather, the climate and natural resources will be controlled by the King of Kings and Lord of Lords and a global planning council of human beings! The debts of countries will be paid off by the Kalki Avatar, as according to Master and talents provision of the Bible! The King of Kings will be the wealthiest and most powerful person in the history of mankind and lead with divine knowledge that leads to a utopian world where there is no more dying, crying, or pain with the help of human chosen leaders! Heaven will be a Kingdom on Earth and God will live forever on Earth and introduce other planets to those with salvation or Moksha on Earth! This is also thanks to Jesus Christ who loved all diverse types of people and was crucified for humanities sins! This also thanks to those who acted as Gog and Magog and Satan for fulfilling the scriptures of all religions because there is a continuous and contiguous relationship between all words and revelations of God! Once the genie is out of the bottle those words must be fulfilled!

Kalki: The Next Avatar of God
and the End of Kali-yuga
by Stephen Knapp
(An excerpt from The Vedic Prophecies)

The age of Kali-yuga is said to start from the year 3102 BC, after the disappearance of Lord Krishna. Lord Caitanya appeared 500 years ago, at which time the Golden Age within Kali-yuga is supposed to start and last another 10,000 years. As the Golden Age within of Kali-yuga comes to a close, the lower modes of material nature will become so strong that people will lose interest in spiritual topics. It is said that everyone will become godless. Whatever devotees, bhaktas, and sages are left on the planet will be so unique in character and peculiar compared with the rest of society that they will be ridiculed and hunted down in the cities for sport like animals. Thus, they will flee the cities to live underground in caves or high up in the mountains, or simply disengage from the earthly plane of existence. In this way, they will disappear from the face of the earth. That is the time when the dark influence of the age of Kali-yuga will become so dominant that its full influence will manifest without hindrance.

Finally, after 432,000 years from the beginning of the age of Kali, Lord Kalki will appear as the twenty-second incarnation of God. This is very similar to what some people call the second coming of Christ.

CHAPTER 17

The Appearance of Lord Kalki

There are many incarnations of the Supreme Being as stated in *Srimad-Bhagavatam* (1.3.26): "O *brahmanas*, the incarnations of the Lord are innumerable, like rivulets flowing from inexhaustible sources of water." However, out of all the various incarnations of the Supreme, the *Srimad-Bhagavatam* (1.3.28) specifically states *"krishnas tu bhagavan svayam,"* which means that Lord Sri Krishna is the original Supreme Personality of God. All others are His plenary portions, or parts of His plenary portions, who descend into this material world to carry out certain responsibilities and to do specific things. This is especially the case when the planets are overly disturbed by miscreants and atheists. In Kali-yuga many years go by in which constant disturbances and social upheavals are allowed to happen, but the Vedic literature predicts that at the end Lord Kalki will make His appearance to change everything, as described in the following verses:

"Thereafter, at the conjunction of two *yugas* [Kali-yuga and Satya-yuga], the Lord of the creation will take His birth as the Kalki incarnation and become the son of Vishnuyasha. At this time, the rulers of the earth will have degenerated into plunderers." (*Bhag.*1.3.25)

"Lord Kalki will appear in the home of the most eminent *brahmana* of Shambhala village, the great soul Vishnuyasha." (*Bhag.*12.2.18)

"At the end of Kali-yuga, when there exist no topics on the subject of God, even at the residences of so-called saints and respectable gentlemen of the three higher castes, and when the power of government is transferred to the hands of ministers elected from the lowborn *shudra* class or those less than them, and when nothing is known of the techniques of sacrifice,

even by word, at that time the Lord will appear as the supreme chastiser."
(*Bhag.*2.7.38)

The *Vishnu Purana* (Book Four, Chapter 24) also explains that, "When the practices taught in the *Vedas* and institutes of law have nearly ceased, and the close of the Kali age shall be nigh, a portion of that divine being who exists of His own spiritual nature, and who is the beginning and end, and who comprehends all things, shall descend upon earth. He will be born in the family of Vishnuyasha, an eminent *brahmana* of Shambhala village, as Kalki, endowed with eight superhuman faculties."

The *Agni Purana* (16.7-9) also explains that when the non-Aryans who pose as kings begin devouring men who appear righteous and feed on human beings, Kalki, as the son of Vishnuyasha, and Yajnavalkya as His priest and teacher, will destroy these non-Aryans with His weapons. He will establish moral law in the form of the fourfold *varnas*, or the suitable organization of society in four classes. After that people will return to the path of righteousness.

The *Padma Purana* (6.71.279-282) relates that Lord Kalki will end the age of Kali and will kill all the wicked *mlecchas* and, thus, destroy the bad condition of the world. He will gather all of the distinguished *brahmanas*and will propound the highest truth. He will know all the ways of life that have perished and will remove the prolonged hunger of the genuine *brahmanas* and the pious. He will be the only ruler of the world that cannot be controlled and will be the banner of victory and adorable to the world.

Here in these verses we find that Lord Kalki will come as a chastiser or warrior. By this time, the planet will be filled with people who will be unable to understand logical conversations. They will be too slow-minded and dull-witted, not capable of being taught much, especially in the way of high philosophy regarding the purpose of life. They will not know what they need to do or how to live. And they certainly will be unable to change their ways. Therefore, Lord Kalki does not come to teach, but simply to chastise, punish, and cleanse the planet.

Furthermore, we also find the name of the place where Lord Kalki will appear and the name of the family in which He will be born. The family will be qualified *brahmanas*. This means that a disciple and family line of spiritually qualified *brahmanas* will remain on the planet throughout the age of Kali, no matter how bad things get. Though they may be hidden, living in a small village somewhere, it will be this line of *bhaktas*, spiritual devotees, from which Lord Kalki will appear in the distant future. No one knows where this village of Shambala is located. Some feel that it is yet to manifest, or that it will be a hidden underground community from which Lord Kalki will appear.

In this connection we find in the *Padma Purana* (6.242.8-12) the prediction that Lord Kalki will be born in the town of Shambala near the end of Kali-yuga from a *brahmana* who is actually an incarnation of Svayambhuva Manu. It is described that Svayambhuva performed austerities at Naimisa on the bank of the Gomati River for acquiring the privilege of having Lord Vishnu as his son in three lifetimes. Lord Vishnu, being pleased with Svayambhuva, granted the blessing that He would appear as Svayambhuva's son as Lord Rama, Krishna, and Kalki. Thus, Svayambhuva would appear as Dasaratha, Vasudeva, and then Vishnuyasha. Also, in the *Padma Purana* (1.40.46) we find Lord Vishnu admits that He will be born in Kali-yuga. Thus, He will appear as Lord Kalki.

CHAPTER 18

The Activities of Lord Kalki

The *Srimad-Bhagavatam* (12.2.19-20) describes Lord Kalki's activities as follows: "Lord Kalki, the Lord of the universe, will mount His swift white horse Devadatta and, sword in hand, travel over the earth exhibiting His eight mystic opulences and eight special qualities of Godhead. Displaying His unequaled effulgence and riding with great speed, He will kill by the millions those thieves who have dared dress as kings."

We should make note here that, as the Vedic literature explains, when the Supreme kills anyone, that person is immediately spiritually purified by His touch and because the person is focused on the Supreme Being while leaving his body. Thus, that person attains the same destination as those *yogis* who spend years steadying the mind in order to meditate and leave their bodies while focused on the Supreme. So being killed by the Supreme is a great advantage for those of a demoniac mentality who would otherwise enter lower realms of existence or even the hellish planets in their next lives.

The *Vishnu Purana* (Book Four, Chapter 24) continues to explain Lord Kalki's activities: "By His irresistible might he will destroy all the *mlecchas* and thieves, and all whose minds are devoted to iniquity. He will reestablish righteousness upon earth, and the minds of those who live at the end of the Kali age shall be awakened and shall be as clear as crystal. The men who are thus changed by virtue of that peculiar time shall be as the seeds of human beings and shall give birth to a race who will follow the laws of the Krita age [Satya-yuga], the age of purity. As it is said, 'When the sun and moon, and the lunar asterism Tishya, and the planet Jupiter, are in one mansion, the Krita age shall return.'" The *Agni Purana* (16.10) also relates that Hari, after giving up the form of Kalki, will go to heaven. Then the Krita or Satya-yuga will return as before.

Additional information that can help us understand the activities of the next coming of God is found in the *Linga Purana* (40.50-92), the *Brahmanda Purana* (1.2.31.76-106 & 2.3.73.104-126), and the *Vayu Purana* (58.75-110). In these texts we find descriptions of Lord Kalki as He will appear in the future and also as how He appeared in previous incarnations as Pramiti in this time period known as the Svayambhuva Manvantara. These texts tell us that as Kali-yuga ends, and after the death of Bhrigu (or in order to slay the Bhrigus), Kalki (Pramiti) took birth in the Lunar dynasty of Manu. He will wander over the planet without being seen by any living being. Then he will start His campaign in His thirty-second year and roam the earth for twenty years. He will take with Him a big army of horses, chariots, and elephants, surrounded by hundreds and thousands of spiritually purified *brahmanas* armed with weapons. [Being *brahmanas*, these weapons may be *brahminical* weapons that are activated by *mantras*, such as the powerful *brahmastra* rather than base weapons of combat such as knives, swords, and spears, or even guns and ordinary explosives.] Though they may try to do battle with Him, He will kill all of the heretics [and false prophets] and wicked, *mleccha* kings.

In a previous incarnation He killed the Udicyas (Northerners), Madhya Deshyas (residents of the middle lands), Purvatiyas (mountain dwellers), Pracyas (Easterners), Praticyas (Westerners), Dakshinatyas (of Southern India), the Simhalas (Sri Lankans), Pahlavas (the fair-skinned nomadic tribes of the Caucasus mountains), Yadavas, Tusharas (people of the area of Mandhata, India, or present day Tukharistan), Cinas (Chinese), Shulikas, Khashas, and different tribes of the Kiratas (aboriginal tribes living in north-eastern India and Nepal) and Vrishalas.

No one could stop Him as He wielded His discus and killed all the barbarians. When He was finished, He rested in the middle land between the Ganges and Yamuna with His ministers and followers. He allowed only a few people to remain, scattered over the planet. These would be as seeds for the next generations that would follow in the next Satya-yuga. Thereafter, when Lord Kalki has made way for the next age of Satya-yuga and delivered the earth and whatever is left of civilization from the effects of Kali-yuga, He will go back to His eternal abode along with His army.

Continuing with the description of Lord Kalki as described in the *Linga, Brahmanda,* and *Vayu Puranas,* they explain that after Lord Kalki returns to His eternal abode, when those subjects surviving at the end of Kali-yuga are enlightened, the *yuga* changes overnight. Then the minds of all people will become enlightened, and with inevitable force Krita or Satya-yuga sets in. People will then realize the soul, and acquire piety, devotion, tranquility, and clear consciousness. Then those *Siddhas* [the enlightened and perfected living beings who had remained invisible on a higher dimension through the end of the age of Kali] return to the earthly dimension and again are clearly visible. They establish themselves with the return of the Saptarishis, the seven sages, who instruct everyone about spiritual life, Vedic knowledge, and the progressive organization of society for a peaceful and fulfilling existence. Then again people flourish and perform the sacred rites, and the sages will remain in authority to continue the advancement of the new Satya-yuga.

CHAPTER 19
The Return of the Golden Age--Satya-Yuga

Herein we can understand that Lord Kalki will simply chastise by killing all of the evil kings and rogues and thereby bring in a new era of enlightened beings, a race whose minds will be as clear as crystal. They will produce offspring that will follow the tendencies of real human beings as found in the age of Satya-yuga.

Srimad-Bhagavatam (12.2.21-24) further describes that after all of the devious and fake kings have been killed, the remaining residents of the towns and cities will smell the breezes that carry the sacred aroma of the Lord's sandalwood paste and decorations, and their minds will then become spiritually purified. When the Supreme Being appears in their hearts in His form of pure goodness, the remaining citizens will abundantly repopulate the earth. With this appearance of Lord Kalki, Satya-yuga will begin again and the remaining humans will produce children in goodness. Thus, when the moon, the sun, and Jupiter are in the constellation Kartaka, Cancer, and together enter the lunar mansion of Pusya, that is when the age of Satya-yuga will begin. Therefore, as related in the *Bhagavatam* (12.2.34), after one thousand celestial years of Kali-yuga, Satya-yuga will again manifest. At that time, the minds of men will be self-effulgent.

The *Vishnu Purana* (Book Four, Chapter One) also relates that the *Vedas* and the principles of *sanatana-dharma*, or the eternal nature of the soul, fade and disappear from the planet at the end of every four ages. The *Bhagavatam* (8.14.4-5) also confirms that there are saintly persons who help reestablish these principles in Satya-yuga along with the basis of *varnashrama*, which is the proper organization of society for humanity. The *Vishnu Purana* continues to explain that it is in the jurisdiction of the seven universal sages or *rishis*(the Saptarishis) to make sure the Vedic knowledge is given currency again, even if these *rishis* must descend from the higher planets to do so. So, in every Satya-yuga the Manu [the demigod son of Brahma who is the lawgiver of humanity] of that age is the author of the body of law, while the sons of Manu and their descendants are sovereigns of the earth. This means that although the genuine spiritual knowledge or Vedic information may disappear from this planet, it is still dwelling elsewhere in the universe, and it is the duty of higher authorities to reestablish it on Earth.

To help in this regard, it is predicted in the *Srimad-Bhagavatam* (12.2.37-38) and the *Vishnu Purana* (Book Four, Chapter 24) that there are two persons who are waiting for the end of Kali-yuga: Devapi of the race of Puru and brother of King Shantanu, and Maru, a descendant of King Ikshvaku. They will be great kings and will help in the process of reestablishing the proper principles in society. These two are alive even now by their great mystic strength obtained through the power of devotion. They have lived through all four of the *yugas* and reside in the village of Kalapa. They are waiting for the end of Kali-yuga. Then, at the beginning of Satya-yuga, under the instructions of the Supreme, they will return to society and be members of the family of the Manu and reestablish the eternal religion of humanity, *sanatana-dharma*, and the institution of *varnashrama*, which is the proper organization of society for its continued harmony in life, and its material and spiritual progress. They will become great kings and form proper governments. Thus, by the arrangement of the Supreme Being, there are those who will always be the guardians of that spiritual knowledge that contains the genuine principles for attaining the real goal of human existence.

After all of this is accomplished, as related in the *Bhagavatam* (12.2.39), the cycle of the four ages of Satya, Treta, Dvapara, and Kali-yugas [a Caturyuga] will continue to repeat itself along with the same general pattern of events.

IS LORD KALKI PREDICTED IN THE BOOK OF REVELATIONS?

Here are some additional interesting points to consider. There are verses from the book of *Revelations* in the Bible that are very similar to the above descriptions in the *Puranas*about Lord Kalki. These verses are so similar that they cannot be ignored and may provide additional insight for Christians and similarities they may share with Vedic culture. In *Revelations* (19.11-16, & 19-21 NIV) it states:

"And I saw heaven opened and behold a white horse; and he that sat upon him was called Faithful and True, and in righteousness he doth judge and make war. His eyes were as a flame of fire, and on his head were many crowns; and he had a name written, but no man knew but he himself. And he was clothed with a vesture dipped in blood: and his name is called The Word of God. And the armies which were in heaven followed him upon white horses, clothed in fine linen, white and clean. And out of his mouth goeth a sharp sword, that with it he should smite the nations: and he shall rule them with a rod of iron: and he treadeth the winepress of the fierceness and wrath of Almighty God. And he hath on his vesture and on his thigh a name written, KING OF KINGS, AND LORD OF LORDS. And I saw the beast, and the kings of the earth, and their armies, gathered together to make war against him that sat on the horse, and against his army. And the beast was taken, and with him the false prophet that wrought miracles before him, with which he deceived them that had received the mark of the beast, and them that worshipped his image. These both were cast alive into a lake of fire burning with brimstone. And the remnant was slain with the sword of him that sat on the horse."

This sounds so much like the incarnation of Lord Kalki that it could hardly be anyone else. Surely, by the time Lord Kalki appears, no one will have the slightest expectation of Him or His appearance. No one will know His name. And His army of *brahmanas* will be as pure as if they had descended from heaven. At the time of Lord Kalki's appearance, He will kill the remaining miscreants and deliver the few saintly people from the present conditions of the earth, changing it back to the Golden Age of Satya-yuga. In this regard, *Revelations* (14.1-3 NIV) also describes:

"And I looked, and, lo, a Lamb [a typical symbol for the Divine or an incarnation of the Divine] stood on the mount Sion, and with him and hundred forty and four thousand, having his Father's name written in their foreheads. And I heard a voice from heaven, as the voice of many waters, and as the voice of a great thunder: and I heard the voice of harpers harping with their harps; And they sung as it were a new song before the throne, and before the four beasts, and the elders: and no man could learn that song but the hundred and forty and four thousand, which were redeemed from the earth."

One significant description in the above verses is that those who are redeemed from the earth will have God's name written on their foreheads. This is a widespread custom of the *brahmanas* in India to write the name of God, such as Vishnu or Krishna, on their foreheads. This is *tilok*, which is usually put on with clay made from the banks of a holy river. We often see this in the middle of the forehead in the shape of a "V" which represents the name of God and that the body is a temple of God, or the three-lined markings of the Shaivites. The Vaishnava mark is made while reciting *"Om keshavaya namaha,"* which means "Salutations to Lord Keshava," another name of Krishna.

So herein could be an indication that when the last of society is delivered from the earth during the end times, they will be those who wear the name of God on their foreheads, at least according to these verses. Also, as in accord with other Vedic prophecies, we can understand that there will be very few people left in the world who will have any piety at all. So, it would fit in with the Vedic prophecies that by the time Lord Kalki appears, there may, indeed, be only 144,000 who will be left in the world worthy of being delivered from the godless and chaotic conditions of the earth. Or these may be the seeds of the new civilization that will start the beginning of the next age of Satya-yuga.

CHAPTER 20

God Would Rather

I know GOD is tired of war, conflict, hate, terror, bigotry, racism, dirty & cynical politics, interest groups, inefficiency, self-promotion, selfishness, corruption, self-aggrandizement, inequality & greed.

GOD would rather:

Resurrect the Dead

Heal the Sick & wounded & physically impaired

Cure the Blind, deaf, mute, vocally impaired & disabled, etc.

Cure the mentally challenged

Beautify the world and restore resources

Mind Cleanse hate & unreasonable or unjustified bias & criminal/sinful thought or behavior out of people

Give wealth to the masses!

Give recourse and restitution to historically exploited and/or oppressed and/or discriminated groups.

Put evil People into Hell/The Lake of Burning Sulfur/Narakam.

I have said this before. Lord Ram, Krishna, Shiva, Brahma or Shakti could not even bring the 32 languages and many Castes of India together! Allah and Prophet Mohammed could not even bring Sunni & Shia of the Muslim world together. Much of the World considers Judaism and the Ten Commandments of Moses to be too insular and Draconian, respectively. Only Jesus could bring the whole world together as he is central to all Abrahamic lineage religions and an incarnation of Lord Krishna/Vishnu according to Chapter 4 Verse 7 of the Bhagavad Gita. Thus, I accepted the Second Coming of Jesus Moniker even though my Hindu friends and relatives mocked me and accused me of basking in the glory, converting out of weaknesses and ego, and even jailed me out of Jealousy. They are not as strategic, conscious, or brilliant and compassionate as I am.

Many Men, Many Men 50 Cent

II thought this would be implied but let me say it clearly. The USA never cared for the plight of people of color or immigrants until my father, D. V. Sastry came here on 3/17/1961. They observed his skin color and his proclivities so the Kennedy's & LBJ, by twisting arms & using political capital and various other power, pass the Civil Rights Act, Voting Rights Act, & Immigration Act!

The Reason JFK is "Moses" & LBJ is "Joshua" is because they brought down the "Walls of Jericho" which is discrimination, bigotry, prejudice, hate, & oppression. This is also why MLK is "Job".

Also, JFK was "Moses the Giver of Laws" because he changed the definitions to make it easier to enter the Kingdom of God. He violated enough of his own Ten Commandments in seemingly acceptable ways that he could allow millions to escape Hell & enter Heaven.

The Lamb/Son of Man is not addicted to alcohol, caffeine or nicotine. The Lamb/Son of Man has stopped smoking, and only started as the signal that was some type of conspiracy with D. V. Subba Rao involved as cigarette smoke was his symbol. It was also a signal to a worldwide network that Subba Rao was alive and well and that the Son of Man/Lamb was in control of things. The Lamb put the cigarette in his mouth on Dec. 23, 2004, on his way to New Orleans as an international signal. Upon reaching New Orleans, there was a snowstorm for Christmas for the first time. The next day after Christmas, there was a Tsunami and Earthquake.

All loyalists to God and the Lamb in the world and all angels in Heaven knew that the Lamb/son of Man was in charge with D. V. Subba Rao (Durvasa Mahamuni/Shiva) because of the Cigarette in the mouth. Thus, the response to these events was proper as former Presidents rushed to raise money for Tsunami relief in SE Asia and India.

Jesus said, "The son of Man comes eating and drinking and you call him a drunkard." (Luke 7:34 NIV). Jesus also said, "All of these must happen," and "no one may take away words from this book (Revelation 22:19 NIV)". The book is "Book of Revelations" and parts of the New Testament which are of specific interest to the Son of Man & not anyone else, thus there can only be one "Lion from the Tribe of Judah with the Key to the Scroll." (Revelation 5:5 NIV) However, to create belief before the judging of the dead and resurrection, many Old Testament prophecies and Vishnu Purana prophecies are coming true also. Thus, the Son of Man must come "drinking "and must be called a "drunkard" as stated in the New Testament (Luke 7: 34 NIV), otherwise there will be NO

HEAVEN on EARTH and NO RESURRECTION. There is a wing of the Republican party that takes these words seriously, while most Democrats would not.

Republicans have kept the topic of God in the national dialog just as similar conservative parties or groups have done in other countries. Thus, the Republicans have understood the Son of Man's dilemma and have decided, they will not worry about the behavior of the Son of Man as long as prophecies are fulfilled and he has the mouth of a lion, eyes of blazing fire, etc.

However, the Democratic Party celebrates diversity, believes in science and evolution, and encourages helping the least of these and attempts to help the poor. The Democratic Party has made the Lamb/Son of Man, an Indian Hindu, feel comfortable in his native land, the United States of America. Democrats tend to let God judge others, execute others, and pass various judgements on others. Some Republicans feel that they should judge others as gatekeepers of the Kingdom of God. The Democrats did not assume they knew how to do this, and which religion was supreme and when to pass judgement on others.

It is obvious form the Senator Larry Craig case, that when it comes to the God, conservative, evangelical Republicans want the Indian Hindu God to actually be a progressive Democrat. The same dynamic holds true in other countries, particularly Democracies. Thus Jesus "comes riding on a Donkey." (Matthew 21:5 NIV)

Believe the reports of President George W. Bush's White House reading the Bible every day. This is what high-level Republicans do. They care more about the Bible than their stupid policy ideas. The Country Club pro-business Republicans are differentiated and can be won over by progressives.

However, remember when you see Republicans acting in coordination it is usually about the Bible. This post will be very controversial! I don't condone men cheating on women. Women are so trusting and so responsible and so loving! I have never cheated on a woman! In fact, women have asked me to mess around and not be tied down! That's usually a bad sign of non-committal behavior.

However, I realized they were doing it for my best interests. The only man who should have multiple loving relationship is GOD weather it is Lord Krishna and his 16,000 Gopikas in the Mahabharata and Bhagavad Gita, The Lamb in the Bible with 144,000 female first fruits and followers, the OLD Testament with King David and his multiple wives, or Quran with Prophet Mohammad and his scores of wives!

However, women are receivers and should not be sexually promiscuous because it is physically and emotionally dangerous. Men should go to prostitutes who are not interested in settling down as a mutually physical release but not a mutually emotional event.

https://www.facebook.com/792238834/posts/10157040145048835?sfns=mo

https://www.facebook.com/792238834/posts/10157040318898835?sfns=mo

https://www.facebook.com/792238834/posts/10157040506123835?sfns=mo

https://www.facebook.com/792238834/posts/10157040790463835?sfns=mo

https://www.facebook.com/792238834/posts/10153331318188835?sfns=mo

https://www.facebook.com/792238834/posts/10156994853918835?sfns=mo

https://www.facebook.com/792238834/posts/10156861500693835?sfns=mo

https://www.facebook.com/792238834/posts/10156875376408835?sfns=mo

https://www.facebook.com/groups/MobileDems/permalink/1551618904923622?sfns=mo

https://www.facebook.com/792238834/posts/10156452997078835?sfns=mo

https://www.facebook.com/792238834/posts/10156424600748835?sfns=mo

https://l.facebook.com/l.php?u=https%3A%2F%2Fwww.bible.com%2Fbible%2F59%2FLUK.7.18-35.esv&h=AT189jiedP4

Jt8aTpjKSH7nDX6Byvu6DCqfgyavoej3XwCQRNecQLYBkfa38DrHPbSI Mp60bcyA4Gh_nfjK19LRAm5-t6vhBd33QDFUVvQ6crPx6d0YjwmyOt5Fp Ar5UyyoTAOw9brb&s=1

https://www.facebook.com/792238834/posts/10157167459448835?sfns=mo

https://www.facebook.com/792238834/posts/10157128841943835/

https://l.facebook.com/l.php?u=https%3A%2F%2Fonedrive. live.com%2Fredir%3Fresid%3DABBFB5335671F297%25214366%26aut hkey%3D%2521ANAv5yT2i6smqko%26ithint%3Dfile%252Cpdf &h=AT03ozXzdzHVRv3H5cHUkCHsOM9k-QcnTZ3vo8XVJxB-XQCBUMv8JdtrmT22GVmtCnY6g5_1XZZv2HvhRtcW0zUeRfqCcVHOU VdltXP4e2R1TaDk1-sCzW1kZyzILmhSFetMWjc5naF2&s=1

https://l.facebook.com/l.php?u=https%3A%2F%2Fonedrive.live.com%2 Fredir%3Fresid%3DABBFB5335671F297%25214390%26authkey%3D%252 1AO888di9sW7vVuQ%26ithint%3Dfile%252Cpdf&h=AT2iknqAkKicJRg6 sXoJqkTGKcTiTmg34GBx2TWf93Vw_PZMHQukgD1tYHC79Zdlh0YBxv jwEF-H4Xp5UE69nz2dVbW2Y0Je3pxW609MkJRqgRocgsXCzhM6Syy4Blla 1L-FpAL4RQoU&s=1

https://l.facebook.com/l.php?u=https%3A%2F%2Fonedrive.live. com%2Fredir%3Fresid%3DABBFB5335671F297%25214383%26authkey% 3D%2521AHJBufSv50LNFBE%26ithint%3Dfile%252Cpdf&h=AT3Yvngw mVD8wckWeJnmy_enTRVZoLqrH3IAvH4I8Jti\V0xTDqDkqXJXCj57P6 cvJ9LWMW9hYoc7vqDJHWHRksvZmOuT6wcsiZT99iDST_JJFJ-AD2_5 GA0I2OhO9kUA0qdskp8Jj7Vo&s=1

https://www.facebook.com/792238834/posts/10157039776963835?sfns=mo

https://www.facebook.com/792238834/posts/10157040790463835?sfns=mo

https://www.facebook.com/792238834/posts/10157005678413835?sfns=mo

https://www.facebook.com/792238834/posts/10156996236938835?sfns=mo

https://www.facebook.com/792238834/posts/10156256117093835?sfns=mo

https://www.facebook.com/792238834/posts/10156251832858835?sfns=mo

https://www.facebook.com/792238834/posts/10156244686978835?sfns=mo

https://www.facebook.com/792238834/posts/10156187378033835?sfns=mo

https://www.facebook.com/792238834/posts/10156179724228835?sfns=mo

https://www.facebook.com/792238834/posts/10156174514813835?sfns=mo

https://www.facebook.com/792238834/posts/10156170463638835?sfns=mo

https://www.facebook.com/792238834/posts/10156084922188835?sfns=mo

https://www.facebook.com/792238834/posts/10155990210953835?sfns=mo

https://www.bible.com/bible/31/REV.11.1-12.books

https://www.facebook.com/792238834/posts/10156900812113835?sfns=mo

https://www.facebook.com/792238834/posts/10156641217913835?sfns=mo

https://www.facebook.com/792238834/posts/10155914180478835/

https://www.facebook.com/792238834/posts/10155909858028835?sfns=mo

https://www.facebook.com/792238834/posts/10155893101453835?sfns=mo

https://www.facebook.com/792238834/posts/10155824224608835?sfns=mo

https://www.facebook.com/792238834/posts/10155802199553835?sfns=mo

https://www.facebook.com/792238834/posts/10155798964238835?sfns=mo

https://www.facebook.com/792238834/posts/10155792418498835?sfns=mo

https://www.facebook.com/792238834/posts/10155739450863835?sfns=mo

https://www.facebook.com/792238834/posts/10155716726033835?sfns=mo

https://www.facebook.com/792238834/posts/10157174391608835/

https://www.facebook.com/792238834/posts/10157310032878835/

https://www.facebook.com/792238834/posts/10157175016123835/

https://www.facebook.com/792238834/posts/10157175015268835/

https://l.facebook.com/l.php?u=https%3A%2F%2Ftimesofindia.indiatimes.
com%2Findia%2Fpm-modis-visit-to-palestine%2Fliveblog%2F62849809.
cms&h=AT2ocVhsKPlK42P2B5QB7y4ej67B9UO6QGZ2SnLlu9h_z9yZ-
T8BpfjJxyROO-HrshHExQwe2ZStnnCZRpu0sIoO8O71LSX2Wt40uUIT9
weyeFUVvMqFU2EXz97sxlBgXT5Z6OpDLy31k-V44-1epxo&s=1
https://l.facebook.com/l.php?u=https%3A%2F%2Feconomictimes.
indiatimes.com%2Fnews%2Fpolitics-and-nation%2Fpm-modi-
arrives-in-palestine-on-a-historic-visit%2Farticleshow%2F62861401.
cms&h=AT2BjFjgBxXVoRaCufSpR9n-bGigSfwaVRTJ-
wnJZgfI2s7J5tyARbHDax1XRIl9a_I0Dm7viZL1JkuNhxwyCcm_
D4xnSDUFr8nnKh4uRu7uagEwS_N_en4klDpyuYD5W4TVuq_
pINdG&s=1

https://l.facebook.com/l.php?u=https%3A%2F%2Ftimesofindia.
indiatimes.com%2Findia%2Fjordans-king-abdullah-in-india%2Fliveblog%
2F63120115.cms&h=AT0RW1K6ZgqtDBFG1LmQAPzj5zSjoowZGJesD
hB_Sn4EAL9Hk58cKFzirux9e30fMkWuAcYwP-b-Jupe-g_iPmAby2Qi2N
HEmqiHwg5XNxjrFaqS0nLMwJ0HaEI6cS6XmqC1YC58mjlri
DPXCSybqys&s=1

https://www.facebook.com/792238834/posts/10155536521648835?sfns=mo

https://www.facebook.com/792238834/posts/10155526103643835?sfns=mo

https://www.facebook.com/792238834/posts/10155495136208835?sfns=mo

https://www.facebook.com/792238834/posts/10155490962673835?sfns=mo

https://www.facebook.com/792238834/posts/10155429323858835?sfns=mo

https://www.facebook.com/792238834/posts/10155375112583835?sfns=mo

https://www.facebook.com/792238834/posts/10155270868018835?sfns=mo

https://www.facebook.com/792238834/posts/10155230459668835?sfns=mo

https://www.facebook.com/792238834/posts/10155213639348835?sfns=mo

https://www.facebook.com/792238834/posts/10155200668618835?sfns=mo

https://www.facebook.com/792238834/posts/10155199832903835?sfns=mo

https://www.facebook.com/792238834/posts/10155162116688835?sfns=mo

https://www.facebook.com/792238834/posts/10155135340563835?sfns=mo

https://www.facebook.com/792238834/posts/10155065384578835?sfns=mo

https://www.facebook.com/792238834/posts/10155056487678835?sfns=mo

https://www.facebook.com/792238834/posts/10154999752198835/

https://www.facebook.com/792238834/posts/10154999410273835?sfns=mo

https://www.facebook.com/792238834/posts/10154984389683835?sfns=mo

https://www.facebook.com/792238834/posts/10154983827293835?sfns=mo

https://www.facebook.com/792238834/posts/10154984389683835?sfns=mo

https://www.facebook.com/792238834/posts/10154948840803835?sfns=mo

https://www.facebook.com/792238834/posts/10154940058218835?sfns=mo

https://www.facebook.com/792238834/posts/10154885112723835?sfns=mo

Dinesh Sastry

https://www.facebook.com/792238834/posts/10154880960333835?sfns=mo

https://www.facebook.com/792238834/posts/10154771112958835?sfns=mo

https://www.facebook.com/792238834/posts/10157013327693835?sfns=mo

https://www.facebook.com/792238834/posts/10157134633948835?sfns=mo

Appendices

Dinesh Sastry's Background in Politics and Business

Dinesh Sastry is a former Trustee of the Democratic National Committee (DNC) and Trustee of the Democratic Senatorial Campaign Committee (DSCC). Dinesh was Chair of the High-Tech Council of the DSCC and was a member of the Leadership 2000 Board for the DNC.

Dinesh has raised Double Figure Millions of Dollars for Democratic causes in past years including the DNC, the DSCC, President Clinton, Vice President Al Gore, Gov. Jerry Brown, Senate majority leader Tom Daschle, Senator Joe Biden, Senator Max Baucus, Rep. Patrick Kennedy, Senator John Edwards, Senator John Kerry, Senator Harry Reid, and others.

Dinesh was one of the top five national fundraisers for the DNC and AL Gore in 2000 election cycle and hosted successful events of $50K per person and $100K per person with President Clinton and Vice President Gore as guests. Dinesh specialized in fundraising from the Silicon Valley and the national Indian-American community.

Dinesh has raised the initial private equity capital for Blackstreet Capital (formerly Milestone Capital Partners) in Washington, DC. This firm was associated with leading Republicans Gov. Haley Barbour and Ed Rogers and founders of the Carlyle Group as well as confidantes of President George W. Bush. Dinesh has been involved with startup and mature ventures in Silicon

Valley, CA, India, and other places. Dinesh has advised a Mid-East based international investment fund. Dinesh raised a majority of the $30 Million Series B round for Ample Communications.

Dinesh devised the strategy plan and executed high level meetings with government officials and military leaders to make the first major US Defense Industry sale to India by helping Thalles Raytheon sell "Firefinder Night Radar" to the Indian Army to be deployed on the Kashmir border. Dinesh did this on behalf of subcontractor Apex Technology And the deal size was $200 Million. This radar system has prevented accidental border wars between India and Pakistan.

Dinesh has launched a dozen Indian channels on the Dish Network Satellite platform in the USA. Dinesh has also launched IPTV services and channels with DishWorld IPTV, now Sling TV.

Dinesh has relationships with many of the top CEO's of Fortune 100 companies including many of the High-Tech name brand companies in Silicon Valley, California. Dinesh is involved with green technology and data analytics and CRM software companies. He is also involved in up and coming sports, fitness, and wellness ventures in India and USA.

Dinesh has been a political consultant in India for leading politicians including Prime Minister P. V, Narasimha Rao, Prime Minister Atal Bihari Vajpayee, and Deputy Prime Minister L. K. Advani. Dinesh encouraged and advised in Indo-US relations during the Clinton and Bush Administrations. In 1998, in the aftermath of nuclear testing by India and Pakistan and subsequent sanctions, Dinesh set up a back-channel exchange of communications between the Vajpayee government and the Clinton administration. This back channel eventually allowed Strobe Talbott and Jaswant Singh to negotiate a detente, normalization of relations, and removal of sanctions on India through official channels.

Dinesh is known as the person who asked President Bill Clinton to become the first US President to acknowledge the South Asian festival of Diwali. Diwali has since become an official White House event.

Dinesh has also had extensive consultations with the Prime Minister Manmohan Singh government, Prime Minister Narendra Modi government in India and the President Obama administration in the USA. Dinesh also informally advises Gov. Jerry Brown of California, USA and Chief Minister Chandra Babu Naidu of Andhra Pradesh, India among others and has stayed in touch with the Trump administration. Dinesh in past was also an adviser to late CM YS Rajashekara Reddy

Dinesh has worked on U. S. Presidential, Gubernatorial, and Congressional campaigns. As an advisor to Gov. Jerry Brown's 1992 Presidential Campaign, Dinesh travelled over most of the USA and negotiated the debate arrangements for Gov. Jerry Brown in Chicago while David Axelrod negotiated on behalf of Gov. Bill Clinton. Dinesh negotiated debates with David Axelrod and Dick Simpson of Chicago.

Dinesh earned a B. S. in Electrical Engineering and Computer Science from U. C. Berkeley and Juris Doctor from Georgetown University Law Center. Dinesh was on the "A" list for Schedule C appointments in the Clinton-Gore administration. Dinesh was elected delegate to California Democratic Party, San Mateo County Democratic Central Committee, and the DNC convention. Dinesh worked as a software and electrical engineer for National Semiconductor, a multi-billion-dollar offshoot of Fairchild Semiconductor, Silicon Valley's first company. At National, Dinesh designed a software product named Mosp that took IBM Mainframe CMS data output and converted that into an input for UC Berkeley "Spice" Chip Design Software.

Dinesh has raised money for and donated to many charitable, spiritual, religious, and cultural non-profit causes and has been aligned with or a member of such organizations.

http://youtu.be/AJ4Wc66JLcY
http://www.presidency.ucsb.edu/ws/index.php?pid=1692
http://economictimes.indiatimes.com/features/the-global-indian-takeover/many-indian-american-faces-are-expected-in-obamas-team/articleshow/3706022.cms
http://m.economictimes.com/news/nri/visa-and-immigration/new-us-immigration-bill-gives-a-leg-up-to-skilled-science-engineering-talent/articleshow/19656005.cms

http://articles.economictimes.indiatimes.com/2008-11-30/news/28465440_1_delegation-britain-and-india-terror-attack
https://www.dropbox.com/s/uf70wpexaup0ted/Emailing%20clash%20Behind%20Closed%20Doors.htm
https://1drv.ms/i/s!ApfycVYztb-rgze3RN1V2pVLIgnb
https://1drv.ms/w/s!ApfycVYztb-rsx7dlTwsBwA5CtjB
http://m.timesofindia.com/city/hyderabad/The-Big-Boys-Club/articleshow/31694812.cms
http://m.timesofindia.com/india/When-former-PM-PV-Narasimha-Rao-gatecrashed-Satya-Nadellas-wedding/articleshow/29965083.cms
http://www.sfgate.com/news/article/Indian-Americans-host-fund-raiser-for-Gore-3055886.php?cmpid=emailarticle&cmpid=emailarticle>
http://articles.latimes.com/2000/oct/30/news/mn-44246

http://www.asianweek.com/2000/10/12/million-dollar-political-muscle/
http://www.hvk.org/2000/0900/90.html
http://expressindia.indianexpress.com/news/ie/daily/20001027/iin27019.html
https://www.dropbox.com/s/rv45h4v1ptawqui/The%20Making%20of%20a%20Democrat%20Kingmaker%20By%20ARTHUR%20J.doc
https://1drv.ms/w/s!ApfycVYztb-rsxM9usqnbLsWlq6a
http://youtu.be/wdOooRVJ0hI

PHOTOS:
https://www.dropbox.com/s/o8j1tc37qmr8qgg/2012-05-14%2019.51.49.jpg
https://www.dropbox.com/s/reg5k7iqbug5ygz/2012-05-14%2019.51.59.jpg
https://1drv.ms/i/s!ApfycVYztb-rgy-XeIil-im2ye6r
https://1drv.ms/i/s!ApfycVYztb-rgyw6mCqgOuqVeekC
https://1drv.ms/i/s!ApfycVYztb-rgytsLneGsanvoh3u

[Company name]

To:	David Axelrod
From:	dinesh sastry
CC:	[Recipient names]
Date:	9/26/2013
Re:	Second Term Election Strategy for the President and DNC

Comments: This is a brief memorandum of some ideas I had that can be expounded upon.

Strategy for Second Term Elections and Governance

President Obama should focus on activities that don't require Congressional action while waiting for the midterm elections in 2014. He can focus on foreign policy and diplomacy throughout the world. His diplomatic skills are considerable, and his foreign policy vision is strategic and encompassing. He can use diplomacy with Iran, Syria, and the Palestinians and Israelis. He can also engage India and China in a way that leads to economic and climate change breakthroughs and relief in Afghanistan and Pakistan.

In addition to foreign policy President Obama can leverage the improving economy and stock market and approach America's top corporations in a strategic and organized way. He can work with them on corporate tax reform, holiday for repatriation of foreign funds, and expansion and employment creation. He should appeal to their patriotism and rational minds. With record profits, these corporations through their highest levels of leadership can be convinced to hire more workers and open more US plants and offices. They can also be forces for Immigration reform. These developments would put the country in a better mood before the midterms. Corporations are profit-driven, rational actors and can work with the reasonable party, the Democratic Party, in an unprecedented way.

Celebrate President Obama's Success

In second terms often the President's successes are not tallied and explained the American people. There is a Frank Sinatra song called "Mr. Success." President Obama should be lauded as a man of success.

For example, he should celebrate:

1. Success in the Stock Market
2. Success in job creation every month for several years.
3. Success in Syria and the chemical weapons avoiding costly war.
4. Success in Iran and diplomacy avoiding costly war.
5. Success in the two-state solution being negotiated between Israel and Palestinians, This will lesson tension throughout the Arab world and Middle Eastern youth and help solve the Al Qaeda recruitment problem.
6. Success in passing Immigration reforms through the Senate.
7. Success in the implementation of Obamacare and the resulting benefits from it.
8. Success in reducing the deficit and national debt since 2010.

Make Argument for Democratic Congress

There should be a clear argument by Democrats in unison and by the President for a Democratic Congress (i.e. retain the Senate and win the House). A Democratic Congress is needed in order to and would allow:

1. President Obama to sign a jobs bill that rebuilds American infrastructure.
2. **Protect and improve** the historic Obamacare law that benefits millions of people.
3. Give the President a strong hang by supporting him in efforts to create a more peaceful world and wind down war and keep America safe.
4. Keep government out of the private lives of women and improve women's rights in the states and federal government.
5. Restore a new formula for the Voting Rights Act and preserve the rights of minorities and elderly to vote.
6. Enact a national background check on gun purchases and limit on ammunition clips.
7. Avoid manufactured crises by the Republican Congress.
8. Govern with Reasonableness and not extremism and recklessness.

Tribute to Obama

All of this can be crystalized by a fundraiser titled "Tribute to President Obama" by the DNC or DCCC. Invite all the corporate leaders to participate along with traditional supporters and try to raise a record sum of money. Stay well-funded for 2014.

Map

Behind Closed Doors

On the presidential campaign trail with Dinesh Sastry

by Manish Vij

Dinesh Sastry, 23, is a rising political star in California. While in college, Sastry took a semester off and traveled the country with former governor Jerry Brown's 1992 presidential campaign. He is now a key campaign staff member for Jerry's sister Kathleen Brown, who is the Democratic gubernatorial candidate. If Kathleen Brown wins in November, Sastry will likely become one of the youngest and highest-ranking South Asian Americans in state government. He is also working with three SAA congressional candidates: Neil Dhillon, Peter Mathews, and Ram Uppuluri.

Sastry grew up in Daly City, California, playing point guard for his high school varsity basketball team. He learned much about politics from his father, former Federation of Indo-American Associations president Durvasula Sastry. Sastry graduated from UC Berkeley this May with a bachelor's in electrical engineering and computer science. In between political campaigns, he hopes to study law, concentrating on intellectual property rights.

Intrigue on the Golden Gate

hum: **How did you get your start in politics?**

Sastry: I started following politics in '84 when the Democratic convention happened in San Francisco. Jesse Jackson was one of my idols at that time. He gave a fiery speech at the convention. Ever since then I've always wanted a Democrat to become president.

My senior year in high school I went hard-core volunteering for Jackson. I met Michael Dukakis and took over a rally happening at the Golden Gate Bridge. I wasn't assigned to do it; I was a volunteer for the San Mateo County Democrats. Me and my friend showed up and crossed these "please do not cross" boundaries. They thought we were sent in by the party. The organizers put us to work. We went in and started coordinating the press corps. I was assigned to be the liaison with the Secret Service. Ted Danson and Daryl Hannah were the two hosts, and Sam Donaldson was there. They gave me a walkie-talkie. I was plugged in right in there, it was so exciting. I wrote about it in my Berkeley application, and everyone in my high school got a kick out of it. The organizers never figured it out. They just thanked us and gave us passes for another meeting.

An unconventional boss

hum: You worked closely with Jerry Brown during his '92 campaign. How did that come about?

Sastry: I've always been an armchair quarterback. I've always wanted to run a political campaign or do sound bites for a politician. My father is a community activist and he's invited Jerry Brown to many events in Northern California. I want to get in on the ground floor and see if I could influence his speeches or his research. I used to go to his house while I was still in school or do odd things, talk to him. Suddenly he decided to run for president. Suddenly the opportunity presented itself right there. Jerry asked me to come on the road, and he asked if I would be willing to take a semester off from school. I knew I'd have an advantage on the road because I'd know him better than the local coordinators. I'd have influence over his scheduling. I became co-coordinator for four states. It was an unprecedented opportunity for someone of my age and ethnic background. Whether Jerry won or lost, he went head-to-head with Bill Clinton. I had an opportunity to meet with Clinton and his advisers, a chance to influence national TV debates. Personal friends don't run for president that often, you have to seize the opportunity when you have it.

hum: **Jerry Brown is well-known for being unconventional...**

Sastry: He's a Gandhian follower. His slogan for president was "Speaking Truth to Power." He took it straight from Gandhi's "Truth is the ultimate reality and has a way of creating power." His idea of running for president and recapturing American government for the people is taken from Gandhi. He says Gandhi succeeded in the movement because, unlike the lawyers of Delhi and Bombay, Gandhi went to the people, to every village. He created a revolution from the bottom up and challenged everyone to become moral agents of change. Jerry even said that when he spoke at the Ghadar memorial.

Age is irrelevant

hum: **Tell me about the televised debates.**

Sastry: In Illinois there were two debates before the statewide primary. I was sent in to do the negotiations. David Axelrod and George Stephanopoulos were representing Bill Clinton. Paul Tsongas had a slick guy representing him. They were wearing suits and were already sitting there with the TV executives. I took the subway and was late. I came in jeans and a shirt. They all looked at me. In their minds they were thinking it's a decoy, the jeans and the shirt, he's actually a shrewd guy.

hum: **They didn't discount you because of your age?**

Sastry: At times I felt young, but all you have to do is throw a suit on. If you can carry yourself well, it gives you instant respect. Put a suit on and speak intelligently and people will respect you. It becomes taboo for them to ask you your age, it becomes an insult, if you speak intelligently. No one would confront me with questions like that. Being a minority, it's hard to tell your age anyway. Besides, there's always a mysterious cloud around our campaign, a respect of the unknown. Jerry Brown does things unconventionally, but he always gets his message across.

Playing poker

hum: **About the debate negotiations...**

Sastry: We started negotiating. Clinton really wanted a sit-down debate. Clinton is good with that. He moves his hands around, never stops talking, and hogs time. I said I want three podiums. The Tsongas guy was waiting and didn't say anything. The TV people asked whether we should allow questions between the candidates. I just smiled. The Clinton people said no way. He was still struggling with Gennifer Flowers, and the S&L scandal was about to happen. Clinton was the front runner, but his people felt he would be very vulnerable.

The Tsongas guy saw that and showed some inclination to supporting questions between candidates. We didn't care, Jerry doesn't give a damn about the format. He doesn't like slick and professional; he just likes to go in and talk.

So, I decided to play games with the thing, I had no preference. I didn't say anything, I just smiled. Stephanopoulos looked at me and said, "Look at the Brown guy, they will go to any length to ask an embarrassing question to Clinton." Right away the Tsongas guy said they wanted questions, and it depends on the Brown guy. I said we might want them. If the Tsongas guy supports three podiums, I'd definitely support having questions. So, he said sure, and it was two-to-one for podiums. The Tsongas guy said we want questions also, and I said sure.

The Clinton guy went through the roof. He wanted to withdraw from the debate. The TV guy said can we have it without questions. The Tsongas guy said no way. I said my preference for questions wasn't that strong. I said there's one way I could be persuaded, if I could get the middle podium for Jerry instead of tossing a coin or picking cards. The Clinton campaign said fine, vote against questions, we'll vote for the middle podium for Jerry. Jerry got the middle podium, which is always an advantage because you're standing in between two guys and it looks like you're being given importance.

When you talk, both men look at you from both sides, and you have a potential for hogging the camera. I also wanted him to be next to Bill Clinton, we'd be going after him hard.

We drew cards for opening and closing statements. We won the first opening statement and traded it for the last closing statement. I knew the closing statement was better for Jerry. He's emotional, and his labor and corruption issues would have a resounding effect.

Clinton goes ballistic

hum: **Wasn't this the debate where Brown and Clinton got into a brawl?**

Sastry: Yeah, the fight was over a Washington Post article. The TV executives sent us a fax saying there'll be no props allowed in the studio. When I showed up for the walk-through, I said we're going to pull out of the debate unless we have props. This was a total bluff; we had no intention of stepping out of the debate. They knew the ratings would dive if we did. The Clinton and Tsongas people said sure, why not, because every other debate so far had allowed props.

On the debate day, Jerry Brown walked in there. Suddenly he raised a newspaper article and said, "Ralph Nader told me something last night that shocked me. Your wife funneled state money into her law firm, and you were involved in the Madison Savings & Loan and Whitewater.

I think you're putting one over on the American public. You have a big electability problem. It's right here in tomorrow's Washington Post."

Bill Clinton went ballistic. He said Jerry didn't belong on the same platform. They started yelling at each other so harshly that the Secret Service got up. Bill was pissed off and created the most dramatic moment of the presidential primary season. Tsongas dropped out five days later because he got no press out of that debate. The cameras zoomed in on Jerry and Clinton. Tsongas was completely ignored.

This year the same TV station called when Kathleen Brown won the primary. They left a message, "This is ABC calling from Illinois. We still think Jerry was the best candidate, and we think you were the coolest and calmest negotiator. If there's anything we can do to help Kathleen, call us up." They all remembered that all this Whitewater stuff started at that debate, and they sent me a copy of the video. I was really proud of that message. I'll never forget it for the rest of my life.

Greasing the machine

hum: **What was the campaign trail like?**

Sastry: You meet movie actors and famous politician. It's rare that everyday people get to meet celebrities in an informal atmosphere where business has to be done. Since we were representing Jerry Brown, they knew we would not mob them, bother them, or ask them to come to a party or abuse their phone number. Matthew Modine took me and a friend out to dinner. I went to a lesbian bar with Whoopi Goldberg. Public Enemy came and did a benefit for Jerry Brown.

I've been a fan of Public Enemy for a long time. Flavor Flave came with his son and said, "Hey, can I introduce my son to Jerry Brown?" Kim Basinger and the B-52's did a benefit for us with MTV hosting it. We had a hamburger together at a bar on top of the club and talked. The B-52's were backstage talking to us. They asked us to send them pins and bumper stickers for Jerry Brown. I met Kevin Costner and Whitney Houston. They came to a rally we were doing while they were filming The Bodyguard. It was very informal, not the big rush you have when everyone's reaching for them, grabbing. I became numb to the excitement of it, it became normal.

hum: **So, who really runs this country?**

Sastry: You might think there are no connections between the rock stars, the conservative businessmen, the movie stars, and the politicians, but at 9:30 p.m.

cocktail receptions behind closed doors they're all moving in the same circles. There's no separation between them. They all represent the top one percent of the wealth and ownership and power in this country. However diverse Public Enemy, Kim Basinger, Ross Perot, Jerry Brown, Matthew Modine, and Walter Shorenstein might seem, you can see them all at a cocktail reception for a political fund-raiser. The money is the lubricant that greases the machine.

From Andhra to N.W.A.

hum: **Have you ever met Jesse Jackson?**

Sastry: Yes, I did. Jesse Jackson was the first person I really idolized in American politics. I put him on a high pedestal. Suddenly I was traveling with him. We went to the site where Martin Luther King was assassinated, where Jackson was standing next to him in Memphis. Jackson took us there. Everything became matter-of-fact after that. If it had happened a couple of years ago, I'd be stuttering in my speech.

hum: **Who are your other role models?**

Sastry: My grandfather is one of my greatest inspirations. He was the most famous criminal lawyer in Andhra Pradesh during his time, and a leader in the Andhra Communist Party. He was fearless. He'd have his supporters sing fiery bhajans and folk songs, angry kinds about oppression. I liken them to the inner-city hard-core rap I used to listen to, NWA, Public Enemy.

In Daly City it's a middle to lower-class area near my schools. Most of my friends were Filipino or black. I've always identified with the lower class, not the rich.

hum: **Do you feel you've faced bias in the political community due to your ethnicity?**

Sastry: I'm sure being a minority has hurt me, but it hasn't confronted me directly. There's no stigma attached to our skin color like with African Americans. I don't think it'll be hard for the Indian community to infiltrate the political community. You need articulateness, persistence, confidence, and intelligence. They'll get good work out of you if you're capable. I predict lots of Indians will go into opposition research, computer types, people who are very quick, intelligent, and resourceful. Indians have been known for those qualities. Campaigns need people like that

hum: **What advice would you give to other SAA political hopefuls?**

Sastry: If you're not in the right networks, you won't get the top jobs in campaigns. You won't get campaign manager or right below that where you're running operations, but you will research issues.

You should start out volunteering and make as many connections as you can. Otherwise it's almost impossible to get a paid job in a responsible position unless you've networked for a long time. As campaigns become more high-tech, they are looking for intelligent university students to do research. Indians can be represented as much as they want to. Like Wall Street, they'll take us because we're good.

Manish Vij

I sent Jerry Brown a long time ago from an old account & computer the articles from Hinduism Today published by Dad's friend at an Ashram/Temple/Monastery in Hawaii about the Irish Celtics & druids & German Nobleman sharing the Vedas with Hindu Brahmins & speaking Indo-European. I told him this would constitute 13 Tribes of "Israel" including Africans. Thus, he started making trips to Europe to study his ancestry in depth. He wanted to see if he is John the Baptist as I stated, could he be related to me in ancient times. I should have forwarded this to more relatives as this would have cleared up the mystery.

The European Nations colonized the Americas after Christopher Columbus set out a sea expedition to find India & buy Indian spices, Gold, & Diamonds & learn the Vedas but ran into America & thought it was India.

India had the most Gold & Diamonds & precious Jewels & wealth in the World. All of Asia was called India at one time. This is why Christopher Columbus called Natives of America, "Indians". He thought he was in the Holy Land of India. That was God's Plan for the USA!

Not that anyone cares but a few stalwart friends want to know why I said Public Enemy # 1, Steve Bannon, and his replacement at Breitbart, Alex Marlow, want such a great man as Jerry Brown as the next USA President despite their RAG'S despicable record of racism, neo-Nazism, fascism and provocation! This is because the late Andrew Breitbart, Steve Bannon, and UC Berkeley's Marlow, consider Jerry Brown to be a Messianic figure that cleans up the MESS created by Bannon & Trump & Pence! They have long considered Jerry to be a John The Baptist like figure before a Kalki Avatar or Second Jesus/ Son of Manu/The Lamb/The Lamp/The Light/Sun figure who rescues the world and makes things right and exhibits the light!

Simply search "Breitbart Jerry Brown" and you will get your answer. Sarcastic, seemingly critical articles concerning Jerry Brown and other progressives that highlight important issues that Jerry and his friends like Willie Brown, George Schultz, and William Perry have dealt with their entire lives in and out of public office.

It is an indirect way for Breitbart followers/readers to be introduced to new issues and a new way of thinking.

The Bride of the Lamb:

Padmaja Gutanka Reddy who also shares the soul of Jennifer Lopez/Olivia Wilde/Madhuri Dixit/Iona Semu/Diane McMahon, Natalie Portman, Indu Magoon, Mary Magdalene/Charlize Theron/Allegra De Peralta/Shamie Samm/Manika Kaur/Lily Singh/Dr. Jyotika Mangipudy/Mother Theresa/Dua Lipa/Rep. Tulsi Gabbard/Jennifer Gates/Aarti Ahuja-UCB/Ileana D'Cruz/Julia Lois Dreyfus/Secretary of State Madeline Albright/Chancellor Angela Merkel/Senator Kamala Harris/PM Theresa May/Danica Patrick/ First Lady Martha Washington/ /First Lady Eleanor Roosevelt/Yvonne De Gaulle/Betty Shabazz/CEO Indra Nooyi/Cardi B/Martha Stewart/Sally Hallon/Betty Gilbi/Dylan Dreyer/Courtney Cox/Riby Rose, Issa Rae, Sukhi Sandhu, Lady Bird Johnson, Rani Mukherjee,/Oprah Winfrey/BessTruman Belinda Carlisle,, Loisa Adams, Merryl Streep, Yoko Ono, Christine Lagarde, Delores Huerta, Carey Mulligan, Nicole Wallace, Ayesha Curry, Bo Derek, Kasturba Gandhi, Constance Wu, CIA Director Gina Haskel, Claire Foy, Preeti Mehra, Reba McEntire, Wanda Sykes, Regina King, Michelle Wolfe, Adele,Anna Kendrick, Taraji B.Henson, Sarah Bareilles, Brie Larsen, Y. S. Sharmila,

Padmaja Guntaka/ Jennifer Lopez is Goddess Lakshmi, Goddess Sita, Goddess Padmvathi, and Goddess Mary Magdalene.

Brides of Lamb/Kalki Avatar (the 18 Shakti Peethas)

/Jennifer Lopez/Olivia Wilde/Madhuri Dixit/Iona Semu/Diane McMahon, Natalie Portman, Indu Magoon, Mary Magdalene/Charlize Theron/Allegra De Peralta/Shamie Samm/Manika Kaur/Lily Singh/Dr. Jyotika Mangipudy/ Mother Theresa/Dua Lipa/Rep. Tulsi Gabbard/Jennifer Gates/Aarti Ahuja-UCB/Ileana D' Cruz/Julia Lois Dreyfus/Secretary of State Madeline Albright/Chancellor Angela Merkel/Senator Kamala Harris/PM Theresa May/Danica Patrick/First Lady Martha Washington/ /First Lady Eleanor Roosevelt/Yvonne De Gaulle/Betty Shabazz/CEO Indra Nooyi/Cardi B/ Martha Stewart/Sally Hallon/Betty Gilbi/Dylan Dreyer/Courtney Cox/ Riby Rose, Issa Rae, Sukhi Sandhu, Lady Bird Johnson, Rani Mukherjee,/ Oprah Winfrey/BessTruman Belinda Carlisle,, Loisa Adams, Merryl Streep, Yoko Ono, Christine Lagarde,, Prime Minister Margaret Thatcher, Delores Huerta, Carey Mulligan, Nicole Wallace, Ayesha Curry, Bo Derek, Kasturba Gandhi, Constance Wu, CIA Director Gina Haskel, Claire Foy, Preeti Mehra, Reba McEntire, Wanda Sykes, Regina King, Michelle Wolfe, Adele, Anna Kendrick, Taraji B.Henson, Paula Abdul, Deputy AD Sally Yates,

(Lakshmi Devi, Goddess Sita)

The other potential 17 Brides of the Lamb & Revelation 14:4 NIV followers of the Lamb:

Mariah Carey/Aubrey Plaza/Susan Rice/Gabriela Von Haugue/ Salma Hayek/Condoleeza Rice/Susan B. Anthony/Actress Sridevi/Shikha Dubey/ Demi Moore/Sarah Abraham/Actress Nayanthara/Vanessa Williams/Singer Adele/ First Lady Mary Todd Lincoln /Shania Twain, Ankita Lokhande, Anna Navarro, first Lady Edith Roosevelt, (Saraswati Devi) /Aishwarya Rai/Celine Dione/Olivia Munn/ Helen Kim//Jennifer Garner/Rupali/ Kumari/Chloe Kim, Angelina Jolie/Shazia Saylab/Kerri Russel, Constance Wu, Rapper Aquafina, Sasha Obama, Jane Fonda, Rep. Ayyana Pressley Senator Kyrsten Sinema,,Abigail Spanberger, Secretary Kirstjen Nielsen, Senator Kirsten Gillibrand, Alarmel Manga(bride of Lord Venkateswara, Katie Nolan, Vidya Balan, (Parvathi Devi)/ Beyonce/Michelle Obama/ Candace Thompson/Kerry Washington /Serena Williams/Jennifer Hudson /Graca Machel/Winnie Mandela/Dedra "Dee" Koch Jada Pinkett, Sen. Amy Klobuchar,Candice Parker, Kim Kardashian//Starr Morrad/ Lakshmi Manchu/Halle Berry/Nicole Kidman/Deepika Padukone/ Whitney Houston/Padma Lakshmi/Sushmita Sen/Ashaki Brown, Pop star Cher, Kiara Advani,/Sharon Stone/Reese Witherspoon/Megyn Kelly/ Jessica Simpson/Le Anne Rhimes/Theresa Hemmen/Alicia Silverstone/ Naomi Campbell/Jessica Alba/Ashanti/Savanah Guthrie/Alyssa Milano/ Zareen Shaukat/Lauryn Hill/Shreya Goushal/Janet Jackson/Shari Headley, Anuradha Paudwal, Carly Rae Jepsen,/Katie Perry/Elizabeth Banks/Edita/ Gwyneth/Anna Kournikova/Melania Trump/Maria Sharapova/Kirsten Bell/Gov. Jennifer Granholm, Shannon Pottoff, Lindsay Lohan, Christina Aguilera, Ziomara Ochoa, Shannon Pottof, Amy Adams, /Julia Roberts/ Madonna/Jessica Chastain/Scarlett Johansenn/Tanja Jevac/Kelly Ripa/Dr. Sarah Long/Janice from Democrats &/Kathleen Brown campaign/Kareena Kapoor/Alexandria Oscasio Cortez/Megan Fox/Kate McKinnon/Natasha Leone/Emma Thompson, Senator Elizabeth Warren, Carla Oringe-DNC, Wendy Williams, Erin Andrews, Nayera Haq, Kellyanne Conway, Marguerite Machen, /Priyanka Chopra/Shivani Sharma/Shakira/Kylie Jenner/Maggie Rogers, ZhalaySarhadi-Pakistani model/Cameron Diaz/Cindy Crawford/ Najia Shaukat/Tyra Banks/Iggy Azalea/Sheila E/Yazmeen Ghauri/Malia Obama/Gretchen Carlson/Miranda Lambert/Nikki Nez/Taylor Swift/Viola Davis/Allison Brie/

Jacqueline Fernanadez/Paris Hilton/Gisselle Bundchen/Lisa Kudrow/Diane Keaton/Fergie/Malala Yousefzai/Bebe Rexta/Marianella Pereyra/Eva Longoria/Mandy Moore/Penelope Cruz/Kate Middleton/ivanka Trump/ Zena Saylab/Marta Obando/Katie Stevens/Karisma Kapoor/Michelle Specs from the Hood/Heidi Klum/Amanda Seyfried/Kylie Minougue, Gayle King, Tiffany Haddish, Ellen DeGeneres, Diane Lane, Queen Latifa,/Swati Narra/ Britney Spears/Jennifer Lawrence/Kim Basinger/Hellen Mirren/Dolly Parton/Kacie Hunt/Catherine Zeta Jones/Nicole/ from our neighborhood/ Amy Adams/Katy Kay/Dolly Parton/Nina Dobrev/ Becky Palter/ Kelly Clarkson/Sandra Bullock/Jennifer Anniston/Allanis Morrisete/Kesha/ Monica Lewinksy/Shagun Chopra/Ipsita Das/Rachel Maddow/Andrea from Hastings Law/Sheryl Crow/Vanessa Williams/Maggie Gyllenhaul, Tracy Ullman, Caitriona Balfe, Christiane Amanpour, Sheryl Sandberg, Camille Ramani, Reshma Saujani,, Bina Erasmus & elder daughter, Drew Barrymore, Maria Butina, Jessica Biel, Huma Abedin, Amal Clooney, Gwen Stefani, Gal Gadot, Norah O'Donnel, etc!, Anna Farris/Meghan Markle/ Camila Cabello/Valerie Jarrett/Sheena Easton, Chrissy Teigen/Ciarra/ Matanga/ M.I.A./Maya, Sarah Jessica Parker, Jennifer Grado, Minka Kelly, Pat Nixon, Ella Mai,Samantha Bee.Abby Huntsman, /Samantha Ruth

Prabhu/ Alicia Keys/Katrina Kaife/Kourtney Kardashian/Maria Menounas/ Alia Bhatt/Kacie Musgraves Eva Green, Erin Burnett-CNN, Selena Gomez, Lady Gaga, Ariana Grande, Nikki Minaj, Rihanna

Why was Lamb/Son of Man dancing and doing other such things a couple of years back?

To some extent, he was humbling himself like a child as in scriptures. However, the main reason he was dancing (though not in a serious or disciplined or skillful way) is because intelligence agencies and Hindus are looking for signs if the Lamb is Lord Shiva and Lord Shiva is known for dancing. Thus, the Lamb/Son of Man put on a dancing show at times. Other attributes and characteristics can be explained as well.

You often see Barack Obama or President Bush dancing recently.

Similarly, Lord Krishna was known for playing the Flute and singing.

People Uniquely Linked to the Durvasula Family

Balakrishna Rao Krovi shares soul of Rupert Murdoch & Dirubhai Ambani

Durvasula Subba Rao (Great, Great Grandfather) shares soul of Morgan (Elder), Winston Churchill, and George Jefferson actor,

Durvasula's share the souls of Ambani Brothers, Tata Family, Birla Family,, Pew Family, Rothschild Family, Vanderbilt's, Google Founders, Twitter Founders, Dulles Brothers,, Rockefeller Family, Chase Family, J. P. Morgan Family, Hearst Family, Getty Family, Ford Family, Audi Family, Mercedes Family, Volkswagen Family (including the many luxury car families bow in this group), DuPont Family, Walton Family, Bezos Family, Mountbatten Family, Windsor Family, Spanish Royals, the Carnegie Family, Walton Family, Walt Disney Family, Nizam family of Hyderabad, the Romanov Family, Founders of Uber & Lyft, Founders of Facebook, Mayo Clinic Family, Drexler Family, BTS-Boy Band.

Durvasula Venkata Sastry (Great Grandfather) shares soul of President Woodrow Wilson, President Dwight D. Eisenhower, John D. Rockefeller, and Henry Ford, Crown Prince of Saudi Arabia, etc. Redd Foxx, Spike Lee,

Durvasula Satya Narayana Murthy (Great Grand Uncle) shares soul of Lord Mountbatten, Eugene Debbs, Bob Marley, King of United Arab Emirates, Jared Kushner, Howard Hughes, James Cameron, John Madden, Redd Skeleton,

Durvasula Venkata Subbarao shares soul of King David, Chief Justice Jon Jay, President Ronald Wilson Reagan, Vice President Henry Wallace, Benjamin Franklin, General Douglas McArthur, Vice President Nelson Rockefeller, Senator Jay Rockefeller, Dr. Martin Luther King, Jr., King Felipe of Spain, Prince Phillip of England, Bill Gates, David Rockefeller, President Zi Jinping of China, President Deng Xiaoping, King of Qatar, Larry Ellison, Steve Jobs, Steven Spielberg, Harrison Ford, Walt Disney, Ted Turner of CNN, etc. many unicorns, William Shakespeare, John Milton-writer, Marlon Brando, Dustin Hoffman, Oskar Schindler, Chandragupta Maurya, Tony Blackman, David Blackman, Governor Elihu Yale of Madras & Yale University,, Clarence Darrow, Willie Nelson, Senator John Glenn, Chief Justice Earl Warren, State Senator Tom Hayden, President Barack Hussein Obama-Surprise!(actor Will Smith, Kanye West, Junior from San Diego, Johnny Wright, William Gist etc.), Trevor Noah, Morgan Freeman, Bill Russell-Celtics-USF Dons, Mychael Thompson, Kareem Abdul Jabbar/Common (rapper/singer), Dwayne Wade, Speaker & Mayor Willie L. Brown-surprise!

Prime Minister Lal Bahudur Shastri, Francis Ford Coppola, David Chapelle, Tom Hanks, Dell Curry, Will.I.Am, President James Monroe, George Lucas, Sundar Pichai, Bob De Maine, Nimitt Mankad, Purvesh Mankad, Craig L. Davis, Manish Vij, Bob DeMaine, Lester Holt, Sen. Bernie Sanders, Craig Melvin, Lester Holt, Biz Stone-Twitter,

Durvasula Atchuthamba (Grandmother) shares soul of Queen Elizabeth, Melinda Gates, Peng Liyuan, Nancy Reagan, Coretta Scott King, Mrs. Dell Curry,

Durvasula Venkata Sastry (Dad) shares soul of President John Adams, President Thomas Jefferson,,Wright Brothers, General Colin Powell, General

George C. Marshall, Sardar Vallabhai Patel, Pope Francis, Sam Walton, a Albert Einstein, Paul Revere, Leonardo Davinci, Justice Thurgood Marshall, Georgia Washington Carver, Edward R. Murrow,, Wolf Blitzer, Mark Felt (Deep Throat), Scholar Laurence Tribe, Steven Ballmer, Warren Buffet (Surprise!), Michael Bloomberg (major Surprise!), Marlon Brando, Robert DeNiro, Bobby Bonds, Akkineni Nageswarao, Jude Law, Michelangelo, Chief Minister Nandamuri Taraka Rama Rao, Joe Lacob-Golden State Warriors, Mohammed Rafi, Mukesh (Singer), Anil Ambani, Actor Krishna, Actor Amithab Bachchan, Actor Chiranjeevi, Producer Dagubatti Rama Naidu, Aloo Ramalingya,, Prime Minister Narendra Modi,

Mother Ramalakshmi Sastry shares soul of Abigail Adams, and wife of Einstein. Martha Jefferson, Saint Katherine Drexel, Evan Williams-Twitter, Arthur O. Sulzberger-NYTIMES

Durvasula Satyanarayana Murthy (Chanti Uncle) shares soul of President Donald J. Trump, George Soros, President Richard M. Nixon, Senator John Edwards, Jack Welch, Jeffrey Immelt, Phi Knight-Nike, Pablo Picasso, Frederick Douglas, Robert L. Johnson-BET, Hedge Fund Manager Robert Mercer, Thomas Paine, President Ulysses S. Grant, Medgar Evers, Jack Nicholson, John Mellencamp, Mukesh Ambani, Jason Alexander (Costanza), Kevin Spacey, Daggubati Suresh Babu, Aloo Aravind, Mike Toomy, Noah Glass-Twitter, Vijay Mallya,

Dinesh Subbaraya Sastry shares soul of Mahatma Gandhi, President John Quincy Adams, Abraham, President Abraham Lincoln, Navy Seal team six member (killed UBL),, Dr. Robert Pepper, President George Wurnashington, President Franklin Delano Roosevelt, President Teddy Roosevelt, Prime Minister Charles De Gaulle, Muhammad Ali (boxer), President Harry Truman, Senator Jeremiah Denton, Justice Oliver Wendell Holmes, Justice John Marshall, Malcolm X, Thomas Edison, Alexander Graham Bell, President Nelson Mandela, Bo Jackson, Al Pacino, Mathew McConaughey, Ingvar Kamprad (IKEA), Carlos Slim, Neil Armstrong, Ludwig van Beethoven, Wolfgang Amadeus Mozart, Rapper Usher, Frank Sinatra, Bryan Cranston, Robert Iger, Gururaj "Desh" Deshpande, John Grisham, Nathan Hale, Wilt Chamberlain, Emperor Nicolas II, Paul Newman, Stephen King -writer,/JP Morgan II,/Rapper Drake, John Mayer, Sumner Redstone-Viacom/CBS, Jeffrey Bewkes-TimevWarner, Reed Hastings-Netflx, A. G.

Sulzburger-NY Times, Stephen B. Burke-NBC, Elon Musk, Ted turner-CNN/TBS, Artist Prince,, David Petraus, Jeffrey Adam Zuckerberg-CNN, President Lyndon Baines Johnson!, Robert Oppenheimer, Henry David Thorough, Cicero, William Faulkner, Sun Tzu, Chanakya/Kautilya, Nicolo Machiavelli, Alex, Kevin Hart-Comedian, Dwayne "the Roc" Johnson, Billy Joel, Jidenna, Ralph Fiennes (actor), Milo Ventimiglia (actor), John Coltrane, Luciano Pavarotti, Mark Twain, Socrates, Plato, H. L. Mencken, John Maynard Keynes, Jimmy Fallon, Satoshi Nakamoto, John Lennon, Richard Gere, Sir Isaac Newton, Booker T. Washington, Benjamn Dubouis, Ricky Gervais, Ernest Hemingway, Galileo Galilei, Vaclac Havel, Nick Jonas, Zubin Mehta, Pandit Ravi Shankar, Rapper Ice Cube, Marc Anthony, Alex Rodriguez, Aloe Blac, Jah-Rule, John Harvard, Amasa Leland Stanford, George Berkley, Henry Durant, Ted Turner-CNN, Jamie Dimon, Lloyd Blankfein, Bob Dylan, Jerry Seinfeld, Adam Smith (Scottish Economist), Fred Astaire, Henry Kissinger, Friedrich Wilhelm Nietzsche, Leo Tolstoy, Little Richard, Elvis Presley,, Jackie Robinson-LA Dodgers,, Aaron Rodgers, Conner McGregor-UFC, Michael J. Fox, Chuck D-Public Enemy, Jim Brown-Cleveland Browns, President Shimon Peres, Bruce Lee, David Carradine, John Stamos, Lenny Kravitz, Prime Minister Menachem Begin, Senator Danielle Patrick Moynihan, Paul Allen, Vin Diesel, Guglielmo Marconi, Anthony Bourdain,, Subash Chandra Bose, George Orwell, Charles Darwin, Charlie Ergen-Dish Network-Echostar, Godfather of Soul-James Brown, MLB pitchers Christy Mathewson & Sandy Koufax, & Nolan Ryan, Singer Tony Bennett, Walter Payton, Julius (Dr. J) Irving, Edson Arentes Do Nascimento (Pele), P. Diddy, Ben Affleck, Marc Anthony, etc.Major Surprise-Quarterback Joe Montana, wide receiver Jerry Rice,, Ervin "Magic" Johnson, Rapper 50 cent (Curtis), Groucho Marx, Karl Marx!, Andrew Gillum, Franco Harris, Christiano Ronaldo, Lionel Messi, Derek Jeter, Willie McCovey, Ronnie Lott, Matt Damon, Bjorn Borg, Boris Becker, LL cool J, Steph Curry, Anthony Davis-Pelicans, Draymond Green, Willie Mays, Barry Bonds, Orlando Cepeda, Juan Marichal, Gaylord Perry, Klay Thompson, Sean Connery, Roger Moore, Pierce Brosnan, George Harrison-Beatles, John Stewart, Mike Kemp, Herschel Walker, Ralph Sampson, Patrick Ewing, Steve Young, Charles Haley, Richard Sherman, John Madden, Brett Favre, Drew Brees, Mario Lemieux, Wayne Gretzky, Fred Dean, Rick the Mailman, Karl (the Mailman) Malone, Chris Mullen, Manny Santos, Manny Hazzard, Denzel Washington, Jim Carey, Jack William Nicklaus-the Golden Bear, Ed Sullivan, Itzhak Perlman, Rob Gronkowski, Brad Pitt, Chris Rock, Special

Ed, Mario Puzo, Nick Jonas, Chesley Sullenberger, Speaker Thomas " Tip" O'Neil, Patrick Mahomes, Jimmy Garoppolo, AVadra,bishek Bachchan, James Packer, Nick Cannon, Akkineni Nagarjuna -Surprise!, Henry Ross Perot, Senator Lloyd Bentsen, Senator Robert M.La Follette Sr.-Wisconsin, Idris Elba, Blake Shelton, actor John Abraham, Founding Father John Hancock, Babe Ruth, Lou Gherig, Johnny Carson, Mark Wahlburg, Post Malone, Reggie Jackson-Mr. October, Levi Strauss, Martin Scorcese, Quentin Tarantino, Bruce Springsteen, Sylvestor Stallone, Hank Aaron from Mobile!, John Derek, David Schwimmer-Friends, David Bowie, Mark Zuckerberg, Stevie Wonder, Joe Namath, Attorney George Conway, Jared Goff-UC Berkeley Golden Bears,-LA Rams, Dr. Dre, Tatum Channing, Singer S. P. Balusubarmanyam, Henry Golding, Attorney David Boies, Jay Z, Caesar Chavez-UFW, Dean Martin, Prince William & Prince Harry, Abhishek Bachchan, Actor Mahesh Babu, Actor Ram Charan, Salman Khan, Shah Rukh Khan,, Actor Pawan Kalyan, FBI Deputy Director & Acting Director Andrew Mc Cabe!!!!!!, John Wayne, Journalist Jamal Kashoggi, Actor D. Venkatesh, Aloo Arjun, James Harden,, Justin Theroux, Founding Father & President James Monroe, Michael B. Hayden, (CIA, Military, NSA), Howard Schultz-Starbucks, Kraft, Jr. etc. Robert Vadra, Rob Gronkowski, Jeff Bezos, Jason Kidd/50 Cent, Robert S. Mueller III, Shaquille O'Neal, Chris Webber, Patrick MacEnroe, Bjorn Borg, Seth Rogen, Sergey Brin-Google, Larry Page-Google, Jack Dorsey-Twitter, Eric Schmidt-Novell/Google/Alphabet, Tiger Woods, Halsey,

Vedantam Durvasala shares soul of Ramakrishna Paramhamsa. Ryan Zinke,

Vinay Prasad Durvasula shares soul of Swami Vivek Ananda Singer/ songwriter Ghantasala, Naga Babu,

Manoj Krishna Sastry shares soul of Christopher Columbus. Trace Thompson, Seth Curry, Jonah Hill, Edward Prichard, Joe Jonas, President Emmanuel Macron, Nick Mullens-QB, Kimball Musk, Kenny G, Prime Minister Justin Trudeau,

Sudhir Durvasula shares soul of Hotmail Founder, Sabeer Bhatia

Kalyan Durvasula shares soul of Kevin Jonas, Hassan Minhaj, Varun Teja (Actor), Daggubati Rana,

Onka Lakshmi Devi (Grandfather DV Subbarao's elder sister) shares soul of Justice Ruth Bader Ginsburg and actress Betty White.& Queen Mother of England., Harriet Tubman, Margaret Thatcher, Harper Lee, Rosa Parks (My favorite), Senator Margaret Chase Smith, Lucille Ball, Fannie Lou Haemer, Stacy Abrams, Audrey Hepburn, Barbara Streisand, Senator Diane Feinstein (surprise! I always thought Gov. Jerry Brown would appoint me to be her replacement even before Jerry became Governor again! However, she never slows down, never retires, just keeps going!), Sydell Curry, Lata Mangeshkar, Prime Minister Margaret Thatcher,

Narayana Rao Chavali shares soul of Sheldon Adelson

Peddapudi Rama Sastry shares soul of Lakshmi Mittal

Lord Hanuman shares soul of pop star Michael Jackson & Michael Jordan (Bulls) & Kevin Durant, Elgin Thomas, Merv Booker (Special Education teacher & basketball coach & scout),

Charles Koch shares soul of Vedantam Durvasula, my Uncle.

David Koch shares soul of Vinay Prasad Durvasula, my Uncle.

Ramoji Rao of Eanadu Group shares soul of my Cousin Ramarao Chavali!

Gov. Edmund G. "Jerry" Brown, Jr. Shares soul of Founding Father James Madison. & President James Garfield, Robert Duval, General Norman Schwarzkopf, Mick Jagger-Rolling Stones, Jerry West, Tom Steyer, President Andrew Jackson, Jerry Lewis, Hugh Hefner, Sen. Cory Booker, Mathew Perry, Todd Owen, Anshumali (Mobile, AL), John Torraco,

Gov. Edmund G. " Pat" Brown shares soul of Patrick Henry,

Gavin Newsome shares soul of Mike Barton, Eminem, Justin Bieber, Vanilla Ice,

President John F. Kennedy shares soul of Nick Pappas, Coach and Officer Richard Hesselroth, Tom Brady, Roger Federer, Larry Bird, Gov. Deval Patrick

Senator Robert F. Kennedy shares soul of Greg Doukis, Douglas J. Band, George Clooney, Brian Williams-NBC, Rep. Beto O'Rourke,

John F. Kennedy Jr. Shares soul of Paul Hesselroth, Chad Fitzgerald, Tom Cruise, Will Farrell etc.

Sen. Ted Kennedy shares soul of Noah Wiley, Jim Murphy, Benjamin Adams, Sen. Ted Cruz,

Johnny Philopopoulos shares soul of Jimmy Kimmel!

Kalyan Kumar Malladi share soul of Nostradamus.

Johnny F. Menese shares soul of Kim Jung Un, Danny Whuo, Jackie Chan, Frankie Rosario, Lou Diamond Phillps, Ronny Cheng,

Hardip Dosange shares soul of Cedric the Entertainer, Wendell Pierce, Anthony Anderson.